1976

DECORATIVE DESIGN
IN MEXICAN HOMES

DECORATIVE DESIGN
IN MEXICAN HOMES

By Verna Cook Shipway and Warren Shipway

ARCHITECTURAL BOOK PUBLISHING CO., INC.

New York

Books by the Shipways

THE MEXICAN HOUSE: Old and New

MEXICAN INTERIORS

MEXICAN HOMES OF TODAY

DECORATIVE DESIGN IN MEXICAN HOMES

Frontispiece:
This early eighteenth-century stone doorway,
a soft pink in color, shows Moorish influence
in the *Mudéjar* convolutions of the arch. It is
flanked by panels carved in the Tree of Life
motif and topped by a pair of primitive caryatids very Indian in conception.

Title photo:
The national emblem of Mexico over the
main entrance to the Museo Nacional de
Antropologia in Chapultepec Park, Mexico
D.F.

Published simultaneously in Canada
by Saunders, of Toronto, Ltd.
Toronto 2B.

Library of Congress Catalog Card Number: 66-18356

Printed in the United States of America

CONTENTS

FOREWORD

This is a book to incite the imagination.

For the aficionado of things Mexican, he can start at the beginning with a most unique and rarely seen "troje" or Tarascan Indian home, from the wooded area near Lake Pátzcuaro. Then, winding his way through long-established haciendas, through urban homes of Colonial antecedents as well as those infused with today's ultra-modernism, he is reminded, again and again, of the timelessness of cultures forming the basis of security and artistry upon which Mexican architecture rests.

It is likely to beguile the architect and the decorator into immersing themselves among the photographs and drawings of honored prototypes as well as their later interpretations, where a wealth of individual design elements are to be found.

This is also a book of ideas.

It may well inspire the home craftsman to exercise his ingenuity. If he is good with his hands, aided by a few tools, an impulse might lead to a sturdy chest with old-looking iron straps and lockplate, or perhaps more simply to gouged door panels of unsuspected naïveté.

But, if paint is his medium, consider the flair given by the addition of stylized or florid designs reminiscent of early frescoes.

For the home owner wishing to inject a bit of Mexican flavor there is, in addition to others scattered throughout the book, a group of thirty-three doors, many detailed, from which to choose the particular character desired. A Moorish geometrical pattern may be preferred, or it may be one with freer floral motifs. Whatever, the replacement of an existing door in an otherwise unadorned wall expanse by one which becomes a focal point is of primary importance in the design of a traditional Mexican home.

So, help yourself freely to the riches of the past which can give to your house decorative meaning.

Our appreciation is rendered to owners of these homes, to their architects, designers, decorators, to the museums, shops and to the craftsmen, each of whom has contributed to the subjects pictured here.

PICTURE LOCATIONS

Below, Spanish names of owners are listed alphabetically by surname or father's name.
Where a following surname is used, it is the family name of the owner's mother.

XII

SEMINARIO de San Martín, Tepotzotlán, Mex.: 27

SEMINARY of the Order of St. Joseph, Apaseo el Grande, Gto.: 147

SOMERS G. Willard, Alamos, Son.: 141
        G. Willard Somers, Architect

STANTON Carl M., Cuernavaca, Mor.: 206, 207

STONE Harry L., San Miguel de Allende, Gto.: 74, 126, 158, 233, 234

TOLTEC Sculpture, Tula, Hgo.: 148, 149

VARGAS Pedro, San Miguel de Allende, Gto.: 204

VILLA Montaña, Santa Maria Hills, Morelia, Mich.: 31, 88, 165, 187, 188, 189, 213, 239
        Ray Coté, Architectural Designer

VILLA Napoli, Mexico, D.F.: 160
        Arturo Pani, Designer and Decorator

VILLEGAS Victor Manuel, Guanajuato, Gto.: 24, 160
        Victor M. Villegas, Architect

WOOD John, Santa Maria Hills, Morelia, Mich.: 51, 100, 104
        Ray Coté, Architectural Designer

YALALAG, Oaxaca, Oax.: 132, 240

GLOSSARY

Italicized Spanish words appearing in the captions are defined below.

ACANALADO .... fluted, grooved

AFICIONADO .... a sport "fan"

ALBERCA .... pool

AMATL .... paper made by Otomí Indians from barks of various trees

ARQUITECTO .... architect

BANDERA .... banner, flag

BAROQUE .... term used today for art style, period 1600 to 1720. Originally from "barroco," meaning irregularly shaped pearl, and used to describe the ornate and bizarre. An outgrowth of Renaissance, originating in Rome. After its transplanting by the Spanish to their American Colonial empire, the Baroque became a true architectural style of the New World.

BARRANCA .... ravine, gorge

BRASERO .... masonry charcoal cooking stove, brazier, a firepan

BUTACA .... classic armchair of Mexico

CABEZA .... head

CALLE .... street

CANCELA............... screening door from zaguán to patio
CANTERA .... quarry stone, stone block
CANTINA............... barroom
CAPILLA.............. chapel
CASA............... house, home
CASITA............... little house, guest house
CATEDRAL .... cathedral
CAOBA .... mahogany
CELOSÍA .... jalousie, window lattice
CHAPETONE .... iron or brass nailheads, at times pierced and decorative
CHARRO............... Mexican horseback rider (who does cowboy tricks)
CHINA POBLANA .... national feminine folk costume, the dress of those
    who dance the Jarabe Tapatío, a legendary Chinese Princess who in-
    troduced the costume
CHURRIGUERESQUE .... a peculiarly Spanish outcome of the Baroque
    style, the utmost in architectural unrestraint and wondrous intricacy.
    Named after José Churriguera, Spanish architect (about 1660-1725).
CINCO DE MAYO .... May 5th: commemorates victory of Mexico against
    the French
CITARILLA .... open fence or balustrade usually built of shaped brick or
    tile
COCINA............... kitchen
COMEDOR .... dining room
CONCHA............... shell, shell ornament
CORREDOR............... gallery around a patio
CRISTO............... Christ, image of Christ crucified
CUESCOMATE or COSCOMATO............... Indian names for a type of silo or
    vasiform granary of clay, found in State of Morelos

DÍA DE LOS MUERTOS............... Day of the Dead. A two-day religious festi-
    val. Feast of All Saints and All Souls Day, Nov. 1-2.

ÉPOCA PORFIRIANA............... lengthy regime of Porfirio Díaz
EQUIPAL .... early chair of pre-Conquest heritage
ESTANCIA............... sitting room, living room
ESTOFADO............... painting on a gilt ground

GANADERÍA .... cattle ranch

GESSO .... coating of plaster of Paris or gypsum for use in painting

GUADALUPE, NUESTRA SEÑORA de .... Patroness of New Spain, Virgin of Guadalupe. The most beloved of all Mexican Santos.

HACIENDA .... estate, large farm, income-producing property

HOSTERÍA DEL CONVENTO .... hostel of the Convent

HUERTA .... orchard and vegetable garden

INTARSIA .... inlay work as a means of decoration, using vari-colored woods

INSTITUTO NACIONAL DE BELLAS ARTES .... National Institute of Fine Arts

LOMAS .... the westerly slope of a residential section of Mexico City

MIRADOR .... a lookout commanding a wide view

MAESTRO .... master craftsman

MARGARITA .... marguerite, daisy, pearl

MARIACHIS .... strolling folk orchestras

MARQUETERÍA POBLANA .... marquetry of Puebla

MATADOR .... bullfighter who killed the bull

MEDIO-PAÑUELO .... one-half handkerchief

MUDÉJAR .... style of architecture or art in the Christian parts of Spain in which Moorish and Italian Renaissance details were seen in the same design

NIÑO .... child, boy

OFRENDA .... an offering to a saint or to the dead

ORATORIO .... private chapel

OBELISCO .... obelisk

PADRE ETERNO .... Eternal Father

PALAPA .... leaf of tree palm, used for thatching; any small thatched shelter or arbor

Glossary

PANES DE MUERTOS................bread of the dead

PARROQUÍA.................parish, parish church

PAPELERA................. near relation of the vargueño cabinet but strictly for papers, documents, writing materials, in that the papelera was minus the hinged front

PASCOLA ....a Yaqui dance, also a dancer of that dance

PATIO.................open court, interior courtyard

PECHO DE PALOMA.................an ogee molding, generally of a beam ending, resembling the plump breast of a dove

PENACHO.................crest, plume

PILA.................basin, fountain basin

PLATERESQUE ....Plateresco period in Spain from 16th to first half of 17th century. Finely scaled decoration derives its name from "plateros" or silversmiths.

POBLANA.................adjective of Puebla

PORTADA.................façade

POSTIGO................. small opening or panel in a door of larger size

POTENCIA .... power, potency, three groups of rays symbolic of the Father, the Son and the Holy Ghost

PUERTA .... door, entrance

PULQUE .... fermented juice of the maguey

REAL SALIDA................. Royal exit or road leading out of a town

RECÁMARA.................bedroom

REJA.................grating, railing

ROSARIO.................rosary

RETABLO.................painted votive offering to a saint who has responded to a prayer

SABINO.................water cypress of Mexico, "Arbol de la Noche Triste"

SAGRARIO .... sacrarium, sanctuary

SALA.................formal room, parlor

SALOMÓNICA.................Baroque twisted column. Name refers to the column in St. Peter's supposed to have come from the Temple of Solomon.

SAN.................contraction for Saint

SANTIAGO.................Saint James

SANTO..................Saint
SANTO NIÑO..................Christ child
SANTO PEDRO..................,....Saint Peter
SEMINARIO DEL OBISPADO..................seminary of the diocese
SERVICIO..................service quarters
SOMBRERO..................hat

TALAVERA.................. glazed pottery made from beginning of 16th century under
        Spanish domination, now continuing in more Mexican character
TALLER ....workshop, studio
TEJAMANIL.................. shingle, small thin board as used in ceilings
TERRAZA..................terrace, open gallery
TEZÓNTLE ....porous building stone from volcanic rock
TIERRA FLORIDA.................. flowery land
TILMA.................. capelike garment worn by men in pre-Conquest days
TORERO .... bullfighter
TORTILLA .... flat, thin cornmeal cake
TRASTERO .... standing display shelves
TROJE..................granary

VIRGEN ....virgin
VARGUEÑO..................Spanish cabinet and desk with a drop-lid

ZAGUÁN .... open passageway through house to patio
ZAPATA..................corbel, short timber placed lengthwise under girder at top of
        post, post-cap
ZEMPASUCHITL .... marigoldlike flower, the flower of the dead

A bearded *Padre Santo* sits on his throne as he awaits the procession in which he will bless the participants and, possibly, one of the *trojes* on the following pages. His robe, enriched with a flowered pattern in *estofado* and shoulder cape in gold with vermillion lining, the dull blue orb and three-tiered tiara, are all attributes of the Christian God as known to the Tarascans.

a rare
Tarascan Indian
home
from the wooded
mountain region
west of
Lake Pátzcuaro

A similar construction in the magnificent new Museo Nacional de Antropologia bears a plaque whose free translation includes:

In the Sierras, the majority of the houses are of wood. The Spanish introduced this type of dwelling. They consist of one single room with a porch along the front. Corn was kept in the loft space to guard it from rats, and because of this these houses were known as *trojes*. The walls, ground and attic floors are formed with thick pine planks. The four steeply pitched hipped roofs are covered with *tejamanil*.

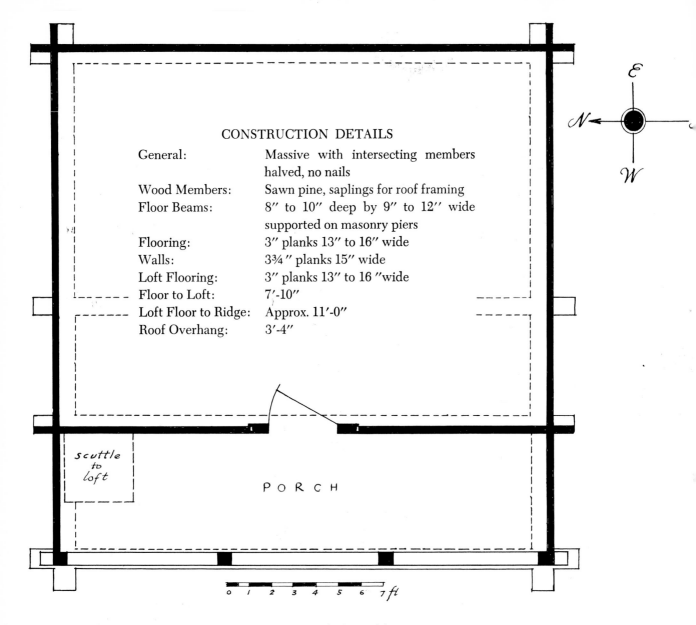

CONSTRUCTION DETAILS

General:	Massive with intersecting members halved, no nails
Wood Members:	Sawn pine, saplings for roof framing
Floor Beams:	8″ to 10″ deep by 9″ to 12″ wide supported on masonry piers
Flooring:	3″ planks 13″ to 16″ wide
Walls:	3¾″ planks 15″ wide
Loft Flooring:	3″ planks 13″ to 16″ wide
Floor to Loft:	7′-10″
Loft Floor to Ridge:	Approx. 11′-0″
Roof Overhang:	3′-4″

scuttle
to
loft

PORCH

0 1 2 3 4 5 6 7 ft

FLOOR PLAN

Rear

End

A *troje* from the vicinity of Paricutín, a village in the State of Michoacán, details of which appear on the preceding and following pages. A cooking area, not shown here, was provided in a lean-to. This example, dating from 1780, has a decided horizontal feeling peculiar to the Chinese in the shaping of its porch arches when compared with the more usual, mixtilinear arches used for others. The fascinating porch posts differ from house to house but all are of the same general character and all are handsomely carved.

The exterior walls had been whitewashed, while under the porch a bit of gayness had been added with pink coloring.

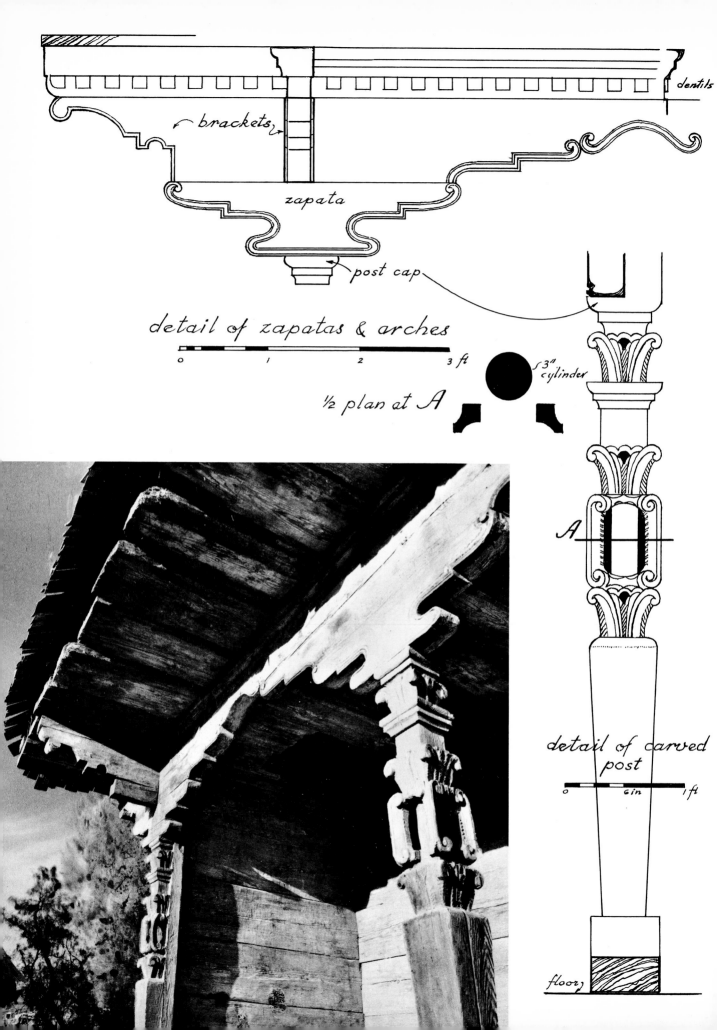

brackets

zapata

post cap

detail of zapatas & arches

0   1   2   3 ft

½ plan at A

3″ cylinder

dentils

A

detail of carved post

0   6 in   1 ft

floor

Left, posts tiered with three modified composite capitals above and below a pierced scroll section are surprisingly knowing in design. Three graceful motifs carved in shallow relief on the lower door panels were apparently considered incomplete without the protective Sun and Moon above.

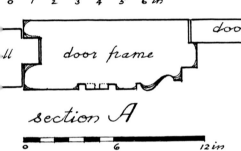

iron strap

section B *C*

0 1 2 3 4 5 6 *in*

door

door frame

section A

0 6 12 *in*

bottom of bed moulding

band of gouged carving

A

B

C

0 3 6 1 2/t *floor*

Looking north from the *troje* previously described to another less elaborately ornamented. Access to the loft grain storage is through the opening in the porch ceiling.

These two pictures show how little variation there was in the vigorous carving of many porch posts. In general, the several elements were more or less similar, but differently arranged. Above is the *troje* in the Museo Nacional de Antropologia. On the face of the center arch an incised Sun is clearly seen and over the right post a horizontal new Moon is evident.

Opposite, a refined example of a *troje* post.

Metepec, a village south of Toluca in the State of Mexico, is renowned for the enthusiastic lavishness displayed by its craftsmen in their many-colored pottery creations. Here, an outsize Santiago is astride a rearing steed, 25″ high overall. This bizarre horse has a white and blue body, decorated with gold motifs, and an orange and black mane.

Santiago is fully equipped to meet any contingency. In gold ornamentation, he has what purports to be a sword in his right hand and a minute shield in the other. A white cape with black and orange motifs flutters from his shoulders while his head is protected by what might appear to be the latest version of the helmets used by the Metepec fire brigade.

10

The hand-loomed wall tapestries of Saul Borisov here and on the two following pages have an inimitable freshness and charm. In this highly imaginative representation of the Ark, Noah and his family are seated under the canopy at the stern. With sails in various shades of red (and different textures) against a red sky, the port rail of this multi-green ship is lined with many types of animals in turquoise and light blue. Four indistinct doves are returning while being eagerly watched by the balance of the animal kingdom along the other rail.

Opposite, using bits of rough woven cotton and a twig, he devised this "Bull's-Head-Twig and Cloth" as the subject of his novel greeting card.

On a tapestry, 24″ x 48″, a golden tiger with black spots gazes pensively around one of the green-leafed, red and blue tulips.

Below, a somewhat questioning and undoubtedly unbrave lion in yellow-gold and black peers from under a leaf, worked in vertical lines of dark olive green.

Borisov

A dark green tree, laden with apples in brilliant reds, yellows and magentas, hides Adam and Eve in shocking pink as they overhear the intimate conversation of the bird and bee, embroidered in the upper foreground on this loomed wool.

13

A majestically treed patio with vine-covered walls is bordered on one side by an arcade. Because of urban encroachment on its former encircling fields, it is now known as *Ex. Hacienda "La Capilla."*

Home of José Antonio García Jimenez

leading from
an existing
street wall
an arcaded
house trails
queue-like
into the
garden

Richly carved panels add elegance to this entrance. Through
partially opened doors can be
seen the undulating wall of the
rear garden and tall cypress beyond.

Home of
Francisco García Valencia

The exterior doors only glimpsed on the preceding page. Each leaf with two equal panels is unusual for Mexico where doors are customarily either of the decorated slab type or multipaneled. Here, the incised floral designs, almost identical, are carved with finesse.

The eight plain recesses between the rails and stiles of the inner faces of the doors opposite were filled, at the owner's suggestion, with incised panels. According to the *maestro* who did the work the subjects depicted are, starting at the top, the Archangel San Miguel, Santiago, patron saint of Spain, San Ramón and, at the bottom Santa Cecilia, patroness of music and musicians. Her authenticity is, however, questioned by some who believe "she" is a "he," a figure of the carver's imagination and more properly identified as "*San Mariachi.*"

Beyond the entrance hall the Garcías have a wide arcaded terrace forming two sides of the more intimate section of the rear garden. The dominant feature is this pool in quatrefoil, eventually to be carpeted with water lilies, while the other two sides are formed by beds of old-fashioned flowers. On the two following pages are other areas of the terrace, both upstairs and down.

For this home, they had again asked their mason *maestro* to form a tree, a very fanciful tree seemingly espaliered on the wall, whose branches would carry their enlarged collection of quaint, small *Santos*. And again the *maestro* has complied, this time with the tree apparently springing from the shaped back of an old bench.

The low parapet wall of the upper terrace carries an almost continuous line of plants, potted only a month or so ago. Later, they will be a colorful headdress in contrast with the severity of the arches below.

A detail of the upper terrace is shown on page 20. The favored tree has space for future growth, the chimney of the master bedroom fireplace ends in a perky little cap of brick and tile and the overhangs of the ceiling beams and rafters are scalloped to give an entirely new effect.

19

Placed between the double doors of the *sala* and *comedor*, the fluted breast carries a delightfully free copy in pink *cantera* of an old communion carving over a mantel of brown *cantera*. The solemnity of the hooded monks forming the legs of the mantel are in amusing contrast with the frisky lambs who tease the double-headed eagle above.

Here, the covered passage from the entrance opens at the extreme right on the other end of the "L"-shaped terrace. In welcome pleasure, the single-brick thickness of the roof slab at the eaves maintains the airy lightness of the arcaded feature. More frequently such roof extensions appear needlessly heavy. The fireplace shown on the left is the focal point around which is concentrated the principal outdoor living area.

21

Home of Francisco García Valencia

Facing page:

An uncommon kitchen, combining the charm of old Mexico with modern conveniences. White walls decorated with garlands of tiny, green pitchers and green-glazed Oaxaca pottery are well lighted through a central cupola above a floor of green terrazo. A brick half-wall forms the inner side of a passage to the kitchen *patio*. At the far end of this passageway, the tan clay stove from Acatlán is a very welcome companion for the breakfast table on cool mornings.

The opening above is centered in the half-wall. These pictures fail to show the other well designed operational areas. That on the left, however, does show, just above the glass jars, not an oversize butter pat but a wood paddle for embossing *tortillas* on festive occasions.

Eleven-inch plates from the *taller* of Jorge Wilmot. The Hapsburg dynasty's double-headed eagle was enthusiastically adopted in Mexico, possibly because in the mythology of some pre-conquest tribes, the eagle symbolized the Sun and the Day. Below, a determined Sun radiates on the Victorian, curtained rim. Both are in shades of brown with soft blue-grays.

Home of Victor M. Villegas

Unpainted, hewn wood members with shaped ends support this range ventilating hood, whose ruffled plaster faces carry up to a sixteen-foot beamed ceiling. The severity of the checkerboard wall, in rectangular blue and white tiles, is relieved by an occasional use of vertical stripes of square tiles, where on pearly backgrounds, Chinese orange birds sit on olive-green sprays.

Home of Carl Renstrom

A swimming pool high above the unbelievably beautiful harbor of Acapulco is serviced by these two areas. One, a large thatched lounge, takes advantage of any breeze while giving protection from the ever present daytime sun. The other is a cooking top of Colonial design in yellow and white medio-pañuela tiles, built in a semi-protected corner of the main *terraza*. Under dark ceiling beams, and on a multi-colored floor of Santa Tomás marble, the combination of the electric broiler and small sink would delight any "cook-out" *aficionado*.

Under a seventeenth-century Spanish wood *Cristo, gessoed* and painted in a naturalistic manner, is this bench, formerly a pew in a church of San Cristóbal las Casas. The rectangular paneling of the back has Moorish roots. The part-figures show how these old wood carvings of religious subjects were sometimes assembled.

Simplicity characterizes this bench with its oddly shaped arm rests and hump-backed finials on the rear supports. Above, a wall decoration of old copper utensils is a part of the pleasant introduction to the *Hostería del Convento*, a part of the *Seminario* de San Martín, that magnificent example of *Churrigueresque* architecture at Tepotzotlán.

Museo Regional de Pátzcuaro

Home of Matilde Ho...

At right: shaped sides with stylized star cutouts support shelves filled with inter-national trophies won by the magnificent Percherons of Holbert Farms.

Modern *trasteros,* or open cupboards, each with a distinctive design. The one above is obviously from the Pátzcuaro area as shown by the ribbed shelf-edging, the finely gouged, circular top, the tableware fashioned from wood and its pottery. *Facing page:* an amusing design from Taxco. Under the nesting birds are several fine examples of *Talavera de Puẽbla.*

Home of Dorothy Macdona...

Museo Regional de Pátzcuaro

A wall shelf, pierced to carry wooden kitchen utensils, is a beautifully executed example of native craftsmanship. The incised carving of the scalloped skirting and of the back is, here and there, accented on the latter by gouge cuts to form a gay, rhythmic floral pattern. This type of decoration, on seventeenth-century furniture brought from Spain, found great favor with Tarascan artisans.

Chocolate beaters, each from one piece of wood are designed to be twirled to thoroughly mix powder and liquid. Turned on lathes, some unpainted, while others, more perfected, are burned, then decorated with finely incised designs and fitted with bone tips.

Two former *cancela* transoms. In that above, with radiating turned spindles, the pattern is free and uncomplicated, while that below has an interlaced center design of delicate, rounded members which is most complex and quite unusual. The encircling band contains carved wood medallions, a form of decoration popular in the Morelia area.

Home of Consuelo B. de Fernandez Cueto

32

Light gray *cantera* voussoirs, separated by salmon-colored brick, form the arches at the rear of the forecourt. Left, a drying yard enclosed by Mexican-pink stucco walls, is capped with *citarillas*; the latter similar to the panel below but without mortar fillings. The entrance door on Page 96 is to the right of the patio wall fountain, while the arch on its left leads to the rear garden.

Jardines de Cuernavaca

The little clay people below, probably symbols of fertility, were found by their present owners years ago when, as week-end excavators, they discovered them on the westerly slopes of present-day Mexico City. About eight inches high, they are thought to date from before 1000 B.C., when they were used by the Haustecas in connection with burials.

Photographs by Guillermo Zamora

On the preceding page, a wide expanse of San Angel and Villa Obregón lies before you from the entrance steps under a cantilevered and suspended, marqueelike covering to the left of the carport seen above.

The home of a hydraulics engineer, Ing. Wade Leandro Rovirosa, has a strictly functional exterior, while the interior reflects its ties with the romance of the past. Exposed and interior steel columns carry the second floor and exterior hard-burned brick walls, painted white. Intentional severity of the architecture is softened by plantings of cactus and annuals in knowing places.

Inspired by carved stone trim of an old Colonial mansion, the panels of this long chest have unusually deep, rich reveals. Only 24″ high but 69½″ in length, with a hinged top, it is both a practical as well as a handsome piece of furniture, traditionally Moorish in appearance.

Artes de Mexico Internacionales S.A.

The entrance from the carport opens upon this broad stair hall with the play room beyond the unusually wide and pivoted, pierced door panel on the left. Off-white textured ceiling, painted white brick, together with deep café au lait plywood walls, red brick floor, cowhide-covered *butacas* and a white cotton rug, are given a vivid contrast of color by the aquamarine of the carpeted stair treads.

The color scheme of the entrance hall is continued through the *comedor* below. Here the aquamarine carpeting is carried from wall to wall. The long cedar table for ten is evenly illuminated at night by the three lanterns, while during the day, light floods in through the glazed ceiling and window wall on the right where a cactus garden strewn with *tezontle* chips provides dramatic interest.

Photographs by Guillermo Zamora

A restored clay conception of unknown purpose and unknown origin, but replete with ancient symbolism.

The planting area on the right side of the entrance hall is below a roof panel of amber and white glass. At the second-floor level, the opening of this inner *patio* is protected by heavy black rails above panels of natural-colored woven rattan.

otographs by Guillermo Zamora

Home of Ing. Wade Leandro Rovirosa

The *Instituto Nacional de Bellas Artes*, during the past few years, has been taking advantage of the varied uses of plastics. The original of this head, known as *La Monumental Cabeza*, is in the museum of La Venta, the ancient Tabasco capital of the Olmecs on the Gulfo de Compeche.

Two meters wide and three meters high, the original, weighing twenty-five tons, is said to have been from the San Lorenzo quarry about eighty kilometers from where it was found. Carved sometime after 1500 B.C., it is the largest Olmec head discovered thus far.

An amusing sidelight: when this apparently ponderous piece of *cantera* was delivered in a lightweight truck, the neighbors were amazed, but when two men carried it into the Rovirosa garden, such a feat was seemingly an act of magic.

39

Rancho Begonia & La Escondida

Two working ranches in the wide valley north of Querétaro devoted to farming, orchards, the breeding of saddle horses and thoroughbreds.

Inside the *patio*, an old pink-stone fountain basin of boldly carved acanthus leaves is the central feature. Varied-headed doors lead to rooms off the shadowed arcade, while at each corner, high on the projecting wall, stands a plumed and musically inclined, diminutive carved-stone Archangel.

Facing page: the main entrance of the restored and massive *Hacienda de Begonia* leads from a walled *heurta* to the *zaguán*. Above tiled benches, religious plaques are placed in the wall under the three crosses of the Trinity.

Below, a wood panel showing six of the Apostles at the Last Supper, three of whom are carved in such relief as to be almost free-standing.

The *hacienda's comedor*, with a twenty-foot-high beamed ceiling, is long enough to permit the seating of more than thirty guests at one time. Orange and white dishes on green and white checkered cloths are overpowered by the ten-paneled screen in the background.

The screen is said to be attributed to Miguel Cabrera, a Zapotec Indian (1695-1768) who, inspired by Murillo, became a leading artist of Mexico, in much demand for church murals. Possibly inspired by romanticism of a later era, nine goddesses, those of Song, Poetry, the Arts and Sciences, "the Muses," are here shown reclining on *Baroque* scrolls set into a dark treed landscape.

A high gallery (*facing page*), screened from the inner court on the left, opens onto the garden area at the right through majestic piers, connecting the old granary ruins which now form a part of this luxurious hostelry, "La Mansión."

One of the many saddles in a tack room of Rancho *La Escondida*. With handsomely tooled leather, embossed silver mounts, a saber with chased guard and a silver linked bridle, this combination would be relished by all *charros*.

A seven-year-old red saddle stallion, "San Jack of Begonia," is led across the stableyard where he stands at stud.

quinta
amayizar

Doors of great simplicity with slightly pillowed panels of French military blue open on a covered passage leading to the main house between open, formal planting areas. The lion-headed, verdigrised brass pulls, with their sympathetic expressions are the dominant decorative features.

Home of Francisco Garay

On the outskirts of San Miguel de Allende and behind a high wall fronting on the historic road leading to Dolores Hidalgo, "The Cradle of National Independence," is this architectural example of neo-classicism.

Overlooking the quiet pool of the central fountain, the two light ash-gray wings of the façade with their regimented windows protected by wrought-iron *rejas*, flank the ivy-coated recess of the entrance. In contrast to the exuberant-design types of *Baroque* and *Churrigueresque* which enrich so many of the early buildings in New Spain, the tranquility of this handsome home becomes a pleasing pause.

Over a refreshingly simple knee-high fireplace, this sun mirror with its gold-leafed rays is an elegant version of a popular decorative piece.

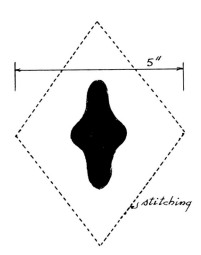

5"

stitching

The rear *corredor* with its white ceiling and deep green walls fairly floats on the reflective surface of its black terrazo flooring. Iron furniture from the shop of the late James D. Ely, painted to simulate the verdigris surface of weathered copper, is upholstered occasionally with white cotton similar to the material used to curtain the arches, a material loomed in the San Miguel mill of the owner.

At left, a detail of the reinforced cutouts which allow enough air to pass through the curtains when closed to prevent excessive billowing.

49

A detail of one of the six wrought-iron *rejas* facing the entrance circle and fountain shows the nicety of its French-flavored cresting.

Here is a lantern graced with decorative flat-iron scrollwork on its cage, mounted
on a bracket of free and vigorous curves.

51

Museo Regionàl de Guadalajara

At the left above, in the *patio* of the *Casa de Juárez*, Oaxaca, an unusual drum-shaped tin lantern with a tier of three collars has a bottom of minute perforations.

Above, a lantern has a patterned tin band at the top of its twenty-six-inch-high cage.

At the entrance to the Harry Brown home, Marfil, a tin lantern with a cresting reminiscent of King Arthur's Court is painted Venetian red.

Essentially the same in design, these two tin lanterns differ only in details. In both the tin cames are minimal. The one below, twenty-three-and-one-half-inch-high, found in a little used section of the Museo Regional de Guadalajara, has an embossed square roof, while the other, hanging from a scrolled bracket over garden steps, has a four-footed shaped base.

The lanterns of Mexico will undoubtedly continue in diverse outlines because of the innate artistry of their designers. Opposite, a handsome hexagonal cage is supported by a pleasingly reversed "S" bracket of wrought iron.

Home of Señora Consuelo B. de Fernandez Cueto

The old *bandera* lantern, twenty-one-inch-high, is glazed in bands of green, white, and red, the National colors of Mexico. Pierced brass members are complemented by lead mountings at the corners of the hexagonal base and at the upper, open gallery.

54

This brass lantern on its chastely formed black iron bracket, is one of the entrance pair on page 57. With characteristics of a carriage lamp, it is a perfect example of how richness is achieved through simplicity.

Galería "Trini"

Home of Francisco Cusi

At left, a processional candleholder used in religious ceremonies is formed with clear glass and leaded cames. The depth between the center panels, spaced to guard against the impingement of flame, gradually decreases until the rosetted tips of the triangular-shaped rays are a part of the circular wire carrying groups of indented leaves.

55

a serene,
satisfying
façade
in
classic
simplicity

Seen from under the wide-spreading branches of an old jacaranda, the approach to this recently completed home of Francisco Cusi in the *Lomas* is by the generous stone stair on the following page.

Opposite, a pinkish tan and charcoal pottery mask of a satyr spouts water into the shallow pool at the turn of the stairs leading to the entrance on this page. The balustrade of light gray *cantera* was based on an earlier example in Aguascalientes.

Under a descending dove and its feathered radiance, both in gold-leaf and both from Spain, this pair of handsomely designed carved wood doors opens into a foyer with marble floor and domed glass ceiling. The pattern of these doors in a slightly changed and less ornate form is used throughout the house to produce a sense of continuity.

In the *sala*, at the right of the foyer, a magnificent crystal chandelier appears even more brilliant against the dark, massive ceiling of wood beams and panels. In the two far corners, *salomónicas* support choicely contrived brass candelabra enriched with colorful Meissen flowers.

The old paintings, three of a series, have to do with the battles between the Ottoman Empire and the Venetians. Starting in 1571 with the victory of Venice at Lepanto in the Gulf of Corinth, the picture on the right records the ultimate victory of the Turkish fleet in 1694.

Offsetting the darker colors of the paintings on the oyster-white walls, the sofa below is upholstered in a bright yellow damask, with motifs in rose-pink and green.

60

Two views of an uncommon dining room. Above a cherry-red rug and eggshell walls, the dark wood ceiling, in general design similar to that of the *sala*, here forms a truncated pyramid. It is topped by a lantern skylight which provides anchorage for the scrolled, horizontal support of the Flemish chandelier.

At the far end of the room (facing page), an arch opens on a glass-ceilinged planting area. The fountain figure in its recessed niche is bordered by luminous panels of colored, leaded glass. The furniture, for the most part, follows the Chippendale tradition. Chairs, made in Mexico, are exceptionally fine copies of a noteworthy prototype.

The buffet, below an amusing oil which purports to be a miscellaneous collection of articles on recessed shelves, truly a "trompe de l'oeil" painted by Salazar Buena Ventura, was one used by Maximilian during his short tenure as Emperor of Mexico.

A radiant plaster *concha* with sharp definition of its surfaces, embraces the master-bedroom entrance. The eggshell white of the walls carries through with a general scheme of grays and yellows, highlighted by the deep blue tones of a handsome collection of Bristol glass. The yellow of bedspread and flounce is picked up in the yellow and green border scrolls of a specially woven gray rug. A dominant feature is the richly shaped and carved headboard, in bronzy-gold.

Between the bedroom and bath, a corridor of doors, adhering to the favored pattern, conceal ample storage-drawer, shoe and wardrobe space. During the day, it is well lighted through the star pierced in its ceiling, and the end bay. The bench of the dressing table is upholstered in the same green and white material used for the draperies and the structural valance above.

Facing page: In a small combination study and guest room, wood paneled, a partially recessed day bed is formally treated with flounce, cover, bolsters, pillows, and even the wall above in black and white tôile-de-Jouy.

A pottery jug from Pátzcuaro glazed over brown and white.

An elegant kitchen based on a composite of Mexican motifs, but far removed from one of earlier days. In general, utensils not in use are out of sight, a condition unknown during the Colonial period. At right, an exterior door separates wide windows over two counter-shelves, each with its own sink.

In the room's center, the robustly curved legs of the cedar table seem in playful contrast to the dominating straight lines. With furniture in clear natural color, the mahogany cabinets are stained a nut-brown against eggshell-white plaster above light olive-green tile. The five and one-quarter inch square tiles above the cooking tops alongside the ovens have yellow borders and designs in greens, yellows, blues and pinks on oatmeal grounds. The *plateresque*, plaster tracery of the dome is in harmony with the cylindrical lantern which seems the work of a silversmith.

Home of Francisco Cusi

A dreamlike bathroom! Sunlight filters through
a ceiling pane and four large pierced stars,
silhouetting the chandelier — a bewitching
bouquet of flowers wrought in iron — to shim-
mer on white walls, gray-veined marble,
French-gray shower curtain, aquamarine tow-
els and accessories, golden octagonal rug,
gilded bath fittings and the two mirrored
walls above opposite marble counter-shelves.

70

A carved stone sprite, inside the glass panel, holds a pot of flowing ivy above the ferns planted along the outer shelf of the tiled tub.

71

Maledictus qui facit opus Dei negligenter. Jeremiae. Cap 48. v. 10.

Mundamini qui fertis vasa Domini. Isaiae. Cap. 52. V. II.

Ingredieris in abundantia sepulcrum, sicut infertur acervus tritici in tempore suo. Job. Cap. 5. v. 26.

With the arched openings outlined in bright pink, the restored frescoes in dark earth-reds, dull pinks and tans all return some of the former elegance of this vaulted washroom of the seventeenth-century Ex-Convento del Carmen, now a museum. The low relief design in gold on a white background decorates the ceiling of the sacristy adjoining the room above.

Shaded blues outlined in black; a vine arbors in fresco an archway overlooking
the altar. From this balcony, screened by a *celosía*, services were seen and heard.

Weathered, grooved beams and ceiling of *tejamaniles* look down on the burnt-orange walls of the *zaguán* and its hexagonal hanging lantern with a foliated, pierced top.

Home of Harry L. Stone

The main stair hall ceiling of the seventeenth-century Monastery of Santo Domingo
in Oaxaca is decorated with plaques and scrolls in low relief, outlined in gold.

75

The vigorously shaped corbels with their gouged volutes add distinction to this construction of exposed walnut beams with grooved soffits. The supported ceiling, shown below at left, is divided into a series of small, flat wood panels outlined by applied moldings. On the right below, a ceiling of square coffers has a built-up panel in the center of each recess, while their slanting sides are decorated with carved, scalloped bandings. Bronze bosses, now verdigris-covered, accent all beam intersections.

Home of Consuelo B. de Fernandez Cueto

Museo Histórico de Churubusco

Above old frescoes, new beams carry a thin brick ceiling. Here, the field pattern as well as the bordering "half-handkerchief" design, is accomplished by painting part in white and leaving the unpainted balance in its natural red color.

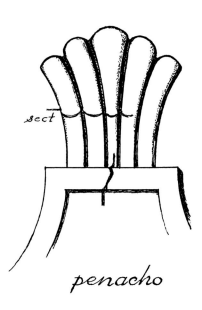

sect

penacho

*Doors from
Home of Arturo Alonso*

Examples of the pleasing effects resulting from the use of frescoes for overdoor embellishment. One is a simple running motif, one is flamboyant in mulberry shades, and the conventionalized design at right is in reds, blues, yellows and soft grays.

80   Beams, stained a light brown, about sixteen inches between, carry this brick ceiling, painted off-white. Lined in diaper pattern, the repeated stylized floral motif was painted free-hand, in royal blue.

The intricacies of this ceiling are in sharp contrast with that opposite. Here, under the choir loft of the church shown on page 82, are extravagant conceptions in cedar of hexagonal and diamond-shaped carved coffers and flowered bosses.

El Convento, Yanhuitlán

Just beyond the choir-loft ceiling on the preceding page, this doorway is a remarkable example of the early use of frescoes to embellish an otherwise nobly proportioned architectural feature. Pronounced among these bountiful decorations are the detailing of the pedimented niche and adjacent flowered areas, the columns painted to appear twisted as *salomónicas* and the repetition of large rosettes on the raised door panels.

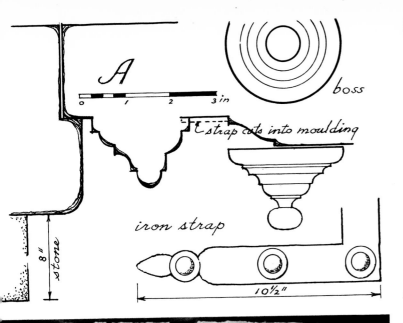

A

boss

strap cuts into moulding

iron strap

10½"

8"

stone

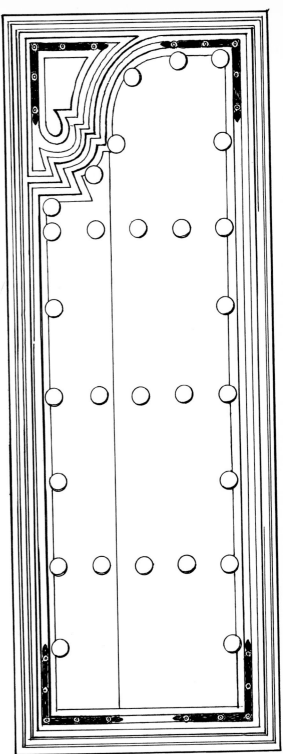

scale in feet

At the entrance to the Jayco shop
is a prototype for many of the
novel door patterns to be found
in San Miguel de Allende.

Under an unusual carved stone shell and two small flower vases, this extremely heavy, old wood grille from a prison, now, with glazed panels, serves a happier use.

86

Simple doors of an old church in Huitzo, State of Oaxaca, enriched by fanciful knockers, structural bosses and two charming draperies carved into the heavy planks.

The older bosses were usually cast brass or iron with cylindrical outlines, while later sheet-metal bosses, stamped and cut in irregular shapes, were sometimes used.

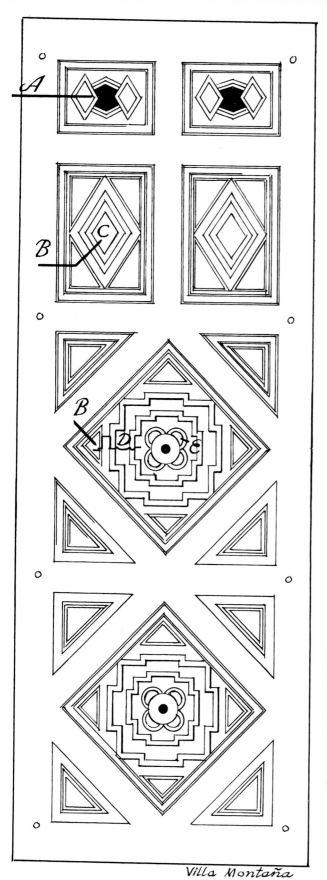

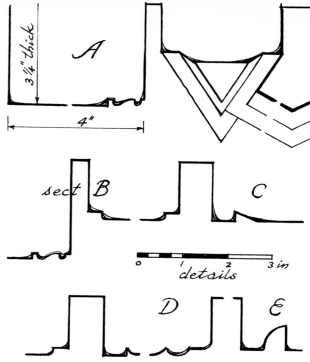

sect *B*   *C*

0   1   2   3 in
details

D   *E*

One of a pair of massive, sixteenth-century doors, only six feet and a half inch high. Except for the petal-like central motif of the middle and bottom panels, the other patterns are strictly geometrical.

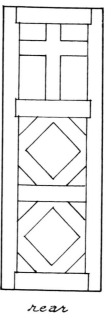

rear

5/8" crate over 1/2" thick panel

Villa Montaña

0   1   2 ft

88

These old and roughly constructed doors close an entrance quite near that shown on page 84. All the crudely run moldings are applied on a flat plank backing. Here, margueritelike bosses were added to the two upper sections for decoration.

A shutter for a window, open to the floor, has panels on which are deeply incised circles and quarter circles flush with the stiles. Above, an earlier shutter which served as the prototype for that on the left.

An old pair of shutters, both hung on one side, with the lower panels fixed and the upper separately hinged for partial ventilation. The beautifully executed floral patterns on the unfinished cedar panels have undergone considerable weathering. Right: one of the shutter *postigos* shown on page 92. Here the details of the carving in high relief can be fully seen and appreciated.

Home of Ray Coté

On the left the outside, and on the right the inside, of a pair of former full-length shutters, each with its *postigo*, now used as entrance doors. The exterior designs are handsomely carved; a simulated marguerite features the two center panels, while in the top and bottom panels, ovals are surrounded by S-scrolls. In each panel, the four shaped and carved corner panels are tongued into their surrounding members. Details opposite.

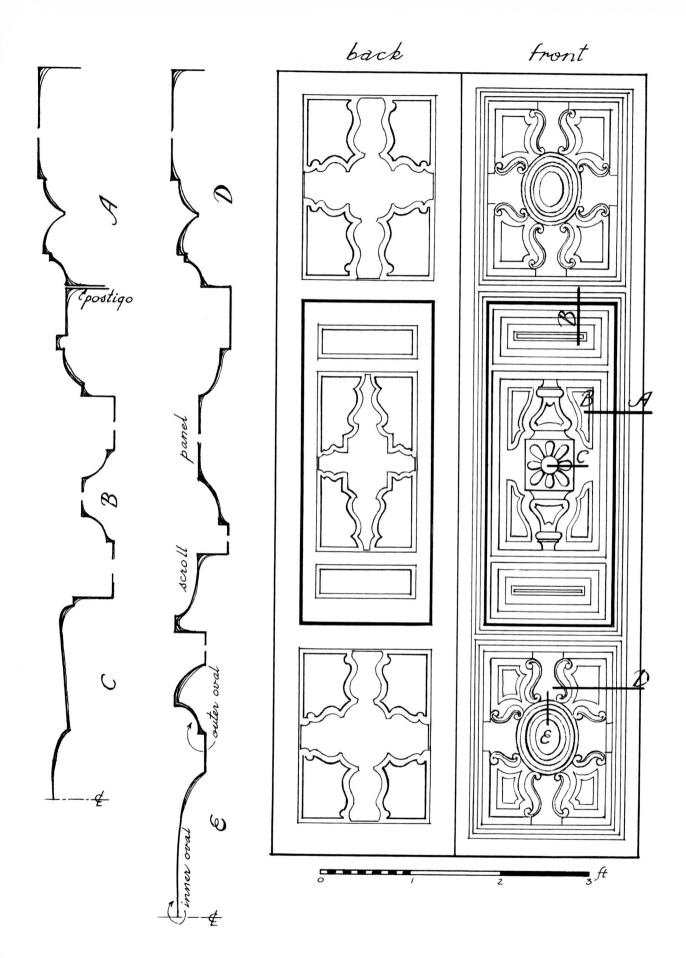

back   front

postigo

panel

scroll

outer oval

inner oval

A

B

C

D

E

A

B

C

D

E

0   1   2   3 *ft*

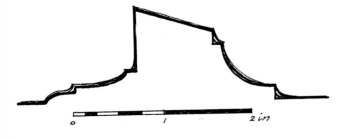

Church of Santa Prisca and San Sebastián

Through skillful combining of moldings and carving, an interesting interplay of light and shade is achieved. The deep panel moldings form an unusual pattern, a truly exciting composition.

94

A few paces to the west of the arch on page 202, a robust old door leaf is one of the many notable designs to be found in Querétaro. The other half is now kept open in order to display the bottles, shoes and papers for sale in part of the former *zaguán*. It is obvious from the richly carved adornment, the shaped moldings, the carefully formed wrought-iron straps and the brass bosses that this was the entrance to a home of distinction.

Home of Consuelo B. de Fernandez Cueto

The exterior and interior of an entrance door, where, true to its Moorish heritage, the craftsman used geometric designs patterned after an early Spanish door. Here all moldings and raised panels are applied. The fresco outlining the interior recess has Colonial antecedents, while, outside, a small and rich mosaic from the Vatican kilns decorates the keystone. The knocker above is on an old Querétaro door. The combination of feathered headdress and luxuriant mustachios is seldom found.

Another door with applied moldings which form hexagonals, stars, and lozenges enjoys a marked relationship with the intricate geometric motifs of the dome-lidded eighteenth-century chest of Mexican construction. The former with lustrous, clear pine surfaces contrasts with the treatment of the chest, where the center of each octagon is painted a deep Indian red, surrounded by carved moldings in black.

Home of Consuelo B. de Fernandez Cueto

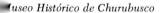

Museo Histórico de Churubusco

97

A cleverly designed door graces the entrance to "La Piña," a shop in La Jolla, California, which specializes in the craftsmanship of Mexico. With applied moldings, both outside and inside, and glass inserts, it reflects the inhibition placed on the Moors by their religion, restricting them to inanimate designs.

Artes de Mexico Internacionales S.A.

Home of Ray Coté

A custom door made to any height and width. The familiar *celosía* pattern makes star-shaped panels enlivened by eight-point wood bosses and forged-iron nailheads. On the right, a pair of doors, each with three raised panels routed from flat boards. A somewhat usual pattern seen on the Continent during the late 1700s but not so familiar to Mexico.

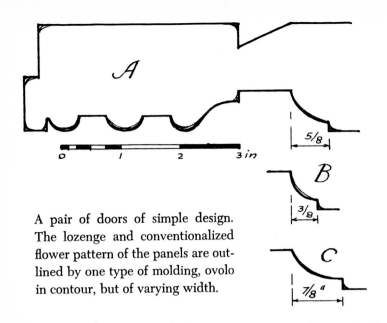

A pair of doors of simple design. The lozenge and conventionalized flower pattern of the panels are outlined by one type of molding, ovolo in contour, but of varying width.

A refreshingly brisk entrance to a Mexico City home under its striped metal ceiling and, then, a handsomely carved pair of doors in San Miguel de Allende; each reflects the translation of the Victorian period, similar to the Napoleon III styles of France. In Mexico, during "La Época Porfiriana," these styles were enthusiastically adopted by the haut monde.

The panels, whose motif is a diamond, closely approximate those above. But, here, the raised triangles and diamonds were run separately and then applied to recessed flat panels.

A

panel

section

elevation

0   1   2   3   4 in

0   1   2 ft

Doors of the Casa Juárez in Oaxaca. An old door above has triangles and lozenges as integral parts of slightly pillowed panels.

Home of Matilda Holbert

A door, whose design is similar to those throughout the house, is here near a small enclosed bar. The panels are outlined by a bead which projects beyond the face of the stiles. The wood has an unusual finish to match that of the old chest shown on page 219.

103

Home of José Antonio García Jimenez

Leading from a storage passage between the shaded *patio* and the rear animal pens of the *Ex-Hacienda "La Capilla"* is this pair of doors, presenting a joyous aspect of carefree design.

When given free play, the imagination of the native craftsman is boundless. On six and one-half inch by fourteen inch raised panels, lizards carved in one-quarter inch relief go slithering up and down.

Home of John Woo

104

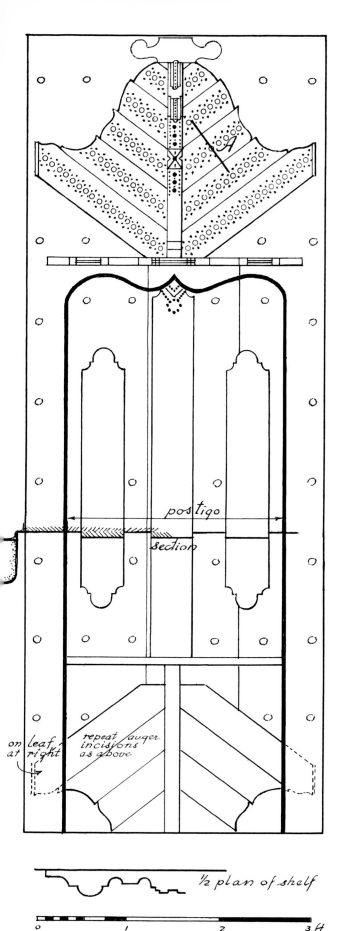

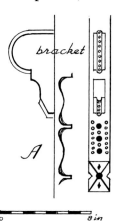

On the highway, Mexico City-Puebla, a two-story home in Huejotzingo has this entrance. The doors, unpainted, with the applied moldings gradually disappearing, are set in a masonry frame painted a soft umber, with surrounding façade a Mexican pink overlay on earlier coats of umber and blue-grays. The detail drawings are a probable reconstruction of the original doors.

postigo

section

on leaf at right

repeat auger incisions as above

½ *plan of shelf*

bracket

A

0   8 in

0   1   2   3 ft

Another pair of old doors where the carving on the raised flat panels is both gouged and incised. Although the treatment of the subject's hair varies somewhat from panel to panel, the carver took obvious delight in portraying the several moods of a single person. They vary from utter disgust in the upper right panel, to disinterest in those of the left leaf, to a pleasurable reaction in the lower right. On the inside surfaces of the recessed panels, each carries the charming circular pattern in gouge carving shown below.

Home of Arturo Alonso

106

Above, one of the pairs of like doors to the twin entrances of the Palacio de Gobierno in Querétaro. Both lower sections swing free to allow for easy foot traffic. The shaped plaques with molded edges are applied on flat, recessed panels and supplemented by carved medallions, decorative brass bosses and iron straps. The knocker opposite, of probable Indian influence, is an arresting mask.

Opposite "La Casa Alvarado" on page 131 is another, equally magnificent door with an unusual panel arrangement. In general, the carved, floral panels in marked relief are similar to those of the doors facing it, but the layout on the hinge side, reminiscent of many shaped door-heads, is quite different.

A remarkable old door, fourty-three inches wide by seventy-six and one-half inches high, has a paneled transom and fixed side panels. The carving in bold relief, floral designs with here and there an added ecclesiastical motif, as the flaming heart near the bottom, is exceptional.

Museo Regional de Pátzcuaro

110   The rosettes, moldings, shaped panels and carved marguerite motifs applied to recessed flat panels give style to this wide pair of gradually weathering doors, facing the *zocalo* of San Martín Texmelucan.

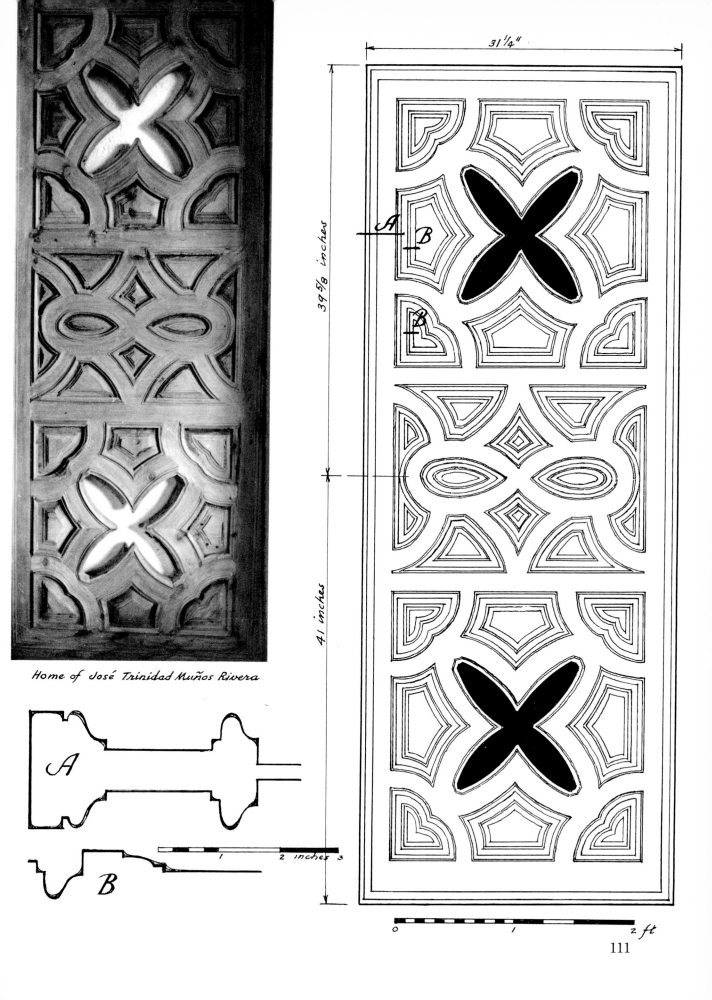

Home of José Trinidad Muños Rivera

31 1/4"

39 5/8 inches

41 inches

2 inches 3

0   1   2 ft

Facing a main street in Cholula, that city of many churches near Puebla, is this pair of doors so charmingly designed in the French manner. Previously painted green, all the applied moldings, plaques and wood carvings are now quite weathered. The delicacy of the cutout designs in the two middle panels has Victorian characteristics, while the half-round molding framing the *postigo* on the left and its counterpart around the fixed panel on the right carry equally spaced gouge-carvings of formal flowers.

Across a tree-filled square, the Alameda León, from the Oaxaca Cathedral stands an old Colonial mansion, formerly the Bishops' Palace, faced with local stone of soft, light green. The elaborate detail of the two-storied main entrance with its handsomely carved stonework is most arresting. Quaint features are two squared blocks immediately above formal Corinthian capitals of highly decorated columns which bear in low relief signs — one a Sun and the other a Moon — so beloved by the natives.

Hotel Monte Alban

While on the keystone of the shaped lintel is carved a scallop shell, symbolic of pilgrimages, above the familiar letters IHS.

The entrance doors are outstanding examples of the type of shallow incised carving found in southern Mexico. By lowering the field only where necessary to bring out the design, a pillowed effect is achieved, subtle and beguiling. Facing are shown these doors in detail.

section A

3 in
2
1
0

postigo

c

motifs cut back
from door face

crate back

5½"

b c b

b

postigo this
side only

A

b

b

0 3 6 9 1ft 2 3 4 ft

115

Fixed side sections with elegantly patterned and pierced panels flank a simple pair of *cancela* doors, whose grillwork is made of iron rods with lead ornamentation.

Home of Ray Coté

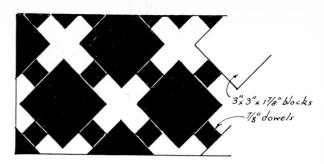

3" x 3" x 1⅛" blocks
⅞" dowels

Examples of wood craftsmanship. One of a pair of spindled and pierced doors formerly blocked the entrance to a Morelia patio from the *zaguán*. And then, a two-leafed screen made up of square wood blocks spaced on short sections of dowels, as detailed above, combining to form an interesting pattern, here used to conceal the kitchen door.

The panel of a ventilated cupboard door with a Moorishlike pattern results from evenly spaced groups of five interlocking auger holes of equal size.

Home of Elton Hyder, Jr.

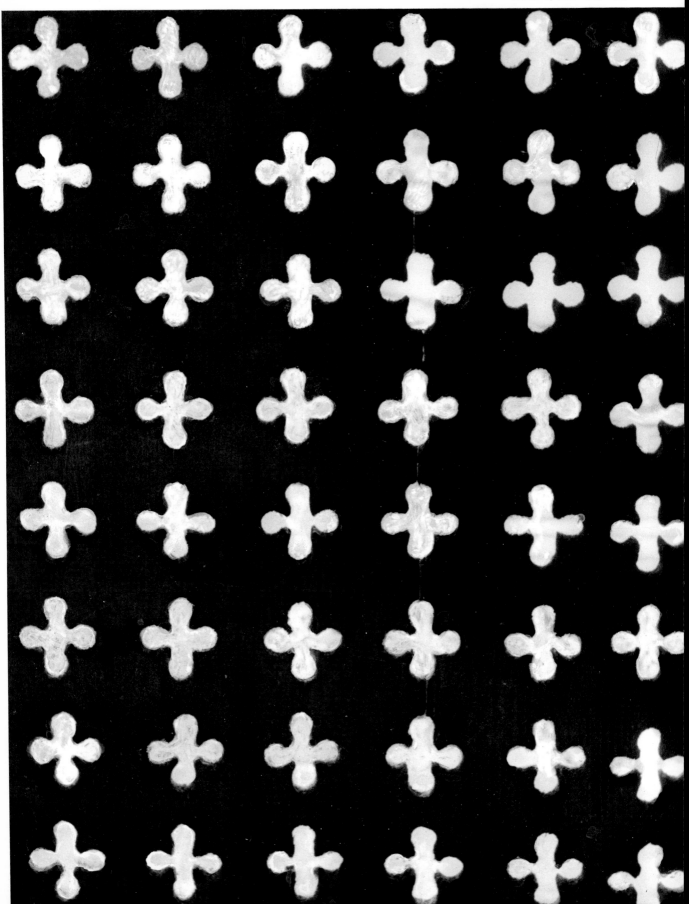

A remarkably well preserved clay figure from the Classic Period of Huasteca Culture, about 600 A.D., found in southern Tamaulipas. Twenty-six inches high, Xochipilli, "God of Flowers," sits here as he probably sat on an ancient altar while a hidden priest projected his voice through the hollow body of the figure from the mouth, the navel and the hands in a religious chant.

Home of Giorgio Belloli

Home of Consuelo B. de Fernandez Cueto

Viewed through an old wrought-iron balustrade, forty-one inches high, the rear garden slopes gradually up to a balustrated stone platform at the far end. The wall above, quite similar to an early aqueduct but here with arched areas bricked in, is very interesting. Over the long stone seat, the two musically inclined Archangels with high Indian *penachos* result from a medley of European teachings and native interpretations.

Home of Francisco Cusi

On this and the following page are stimulating paving treatments, all formed with substantially the same materials — white marble chips and smooth pebbles, ovate and rounded, set in brushed-out cement beds. Those above are on platforms of the stairs ascending from the street portal. Below, a garage apron and the sidewalk fronting the property.

Home of Matilde Holbert

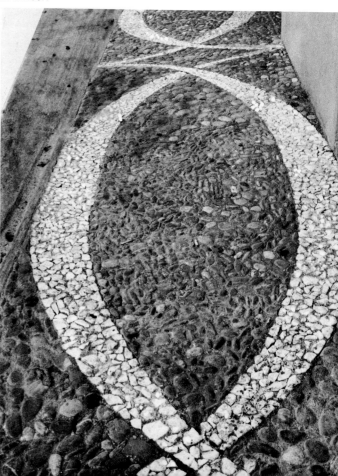

Here, a ruglike effect. Brick tiles shaped in outline have been added to the inner border. Red pan roofing tile on edge surrounded by marble chips alternate with panels of peened gray flagstone. The outer border consists of two rows of square flagstone between marble chips.

In an open gardened recess, *Santiago,* the patron saint of Spain, and worshiped by the primitive Indians of New Spain as a war god, guards the adjacent *patio* entrance. Carved from gray *cantera,* rider and horse are separate pieces. The enclosing wall of adobe brick is enlivened by the salmon-pink tile chips which dot the mortar joints.

Home of Arturo Alonso

Home of Althea Revere

Property limitations and a great pepper tree combined to require considerable ingenuity in the planning of an unobstrusive masonry stair to the balcony of a guest bedroom. With one curved and three straight runs, the problem was solved.

125

Home of Paul Barnes

The lushly planted *patio* of *Casa del Obelisco*
is entered at the extreme right, through the *zaguán* pictured on page 74. The open dining area,
behind the well proportioned chocolate-colored
stone columns of the short "L"-shaped *arcade*,
looks out over the brown fountain with pool, surrounded by an ever changing background of light
and shade.

Above: across the shimmering water surface of
an old stone *pila*, toward an iron stair in a far
corner of the *patio*. With little space, a tight
spiral was required to gain access to the studio
above the guest rooms.

A right turn after passing through the entrance gates and *patio* on the following page leads to the stableyard. A round and well ventilated hay storage forms a base for the many-windowed studio-dressing room.

128

Home of Leonardo Obregón Formoso

Immediately off a busy street in Tlacopac, Villa Obregón, an impressive cypress-lined private avenue ends at this arch of radiating brick tile. In seconds one is transported into seductive tranquillity.

Mottled by afternoon shadows, a pair of old plank doors guards an opening in the wall alongside the present church dedicated to St. Matthew in Churubusco. The brightly polished brass bosses are their only adornment. The use of tile coping to form rough scrolls at the ends of the shaped pediment is particularly interesting.

On house façades, the use of plaster to form geometrical patterns in low relief was a feature of the *Plateresque*. On this famous old home, the raised design is in buff on a background of weathered Mexican pink.

Except for the carved wood astragal and bronze knocker, the magnificent doors below with their varied floral, carved panels are similar to the lower sections of the doors at the side entrance to *El Sagrario*, built around 1750, adjoining *La Catedral* in the City of Mexico.

Home of Thomas Briscoe Miller

Over the years, Mexicans have, in general, been fatalists. "*El Dia de los Muertos,* November 2, is a national holiday. For days before and after, death is everywhere present. He leers invitingly from bakery windows, where there are special *panes de muertos* or the bread of the dead in animal and human forms; from candy shops, in skulls with bright tinsel eyes."

from Mexican Folkways, by
Frances Toor

On the right, Jesús Reyes Ferreira, that inspiring Mexican artist, has designed this primitive wood carving, twenty-eight and one-half inches high, suggested by a baker's confection for the Day of the Dead. First painted white with an overlay of magenta, mostly rubbed off, it will be a model for a window of a local cemetery chapel.

On the preceding page, an unusual *ofrenda* is housed in a red open-back case, thirty-one inches high. All articles are carved from wood in imitation of the real *ofrendas.* Below a proscenium with applied yellow *zempasuchitl* flowers, San Pedro holds the key to Heaven and, surrounded by four archangels, looks out over the food offerings prepared by the living for the returning souls of the dead.

airily practical where gracious
living lies within its walls

Home of Irvin Hovgaard

Announced by the mission bell hung from its star-pierced beam high on the street wall, a forecourt is entered whose curved, flagged walk leads past a fountain to the main entrance opening upon the *terraza*.

Here, a sweeping view opens; the main wing of the three walled *terraza* to the left, the inner garden with an inviting *alberca* ahead and to the right, and then, in the far distance, snow-capped mountains. Plants potted in glazed clay urns form a border along the open south side of this outdoor living area. The whole is given added zest by the vibrant purples, greens, tans, yellows and Mexican pink of the cushions and upholstery of the natural-finished white cedar furniture used throughout the home.

The *sala,* enclosed on three sides by masonry walls, is graced with over-all daylight. It streams through amber and white glass over the planting bed to the right, through the lantern at the top of the pyramidal ceiling, and through the wall of glass facing the forecourt entrance.

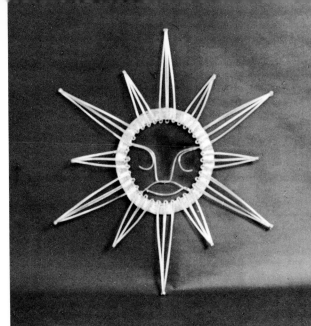

This is the street wall of the *co-cina* whose plan is on the following page. The knowledge-able working requirements of the owners and the inherited influences of the designer were coupled to produce a Colonial kitchen of exceptional individu-ality.

Above a series of gas burners (instead of the old fashioned charcoal brasiers) the wall of lustrous tile is the background for a fluted ventilating hood, re-mindful of one in an eighteenth-century *hacienda* west of Queré-taro. The hood shelf, garlanded with swags of garlic, carries rep-resentative pottery pieces from Oaxaca, Michoacán and Puebla, both useful and decorative. A large cupola in the center of the barrel ceiling, together with four large pierced stars, two of which are shown, provides unusually good, uniform lighting, despite the absence of windows. An ex-ample of the thoughtful plan-ning is the convenience of hav-ing a small washbowl close at hand when working with pastry.

137

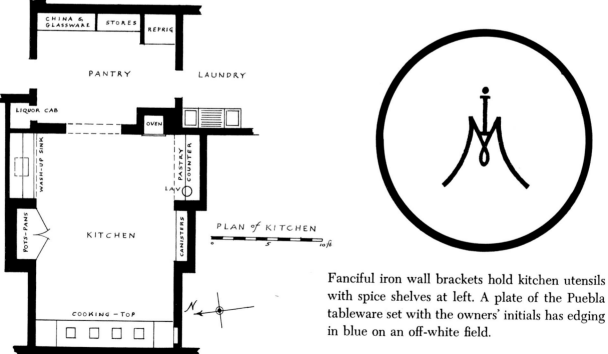

CHINA & GLASSWARE | STORES | REFRIG

PANTRY   LAUNDRY

LIQUOR CAB

OVEN

WASH-UP SINK

POTS-PANS

KITCHEN

LAV

PASTRY COUNTER

CANISTERS

PLAN of KITCHEN

0   5   10 ft

COOKING-TOP

N

Fanciful iron wall brackets hold kitchen utensils with spice shelves at left. A plate of the Puebla tableware set with the owners' initials has edging in blue on an off-white field.

Home of Irvin Hovgaard

Home of José Trinidad Muñoz Rivera

In the westerly wall between the *terraza* and the forecourt a carved stone opening, surrounded by a luxuriant green vine, contains a musically inclined guitar-playing archangel inspired by the left figure over *La Puerta Colonial de La Parroquía* of Yuriría.

An attentive, intelligent-looking dog of uncertain breed and sex, with a body from a single piece of wood. The wide back is available for use as a small bench or magazine shelf.

139

140   This wrought-iron tracery, with its unique, heart-shaped motifs and center radia-
tions, is a transom over the entrance hall leading to the sunlit *patio* beyond.

The second-floor window of an old house under reconstruction has a *reja* unusually deep to accommodate the outswinging screens. The closed head with its pleasing outline is accented by small wrought-iron curlicues.

Home of G. Willard Somers

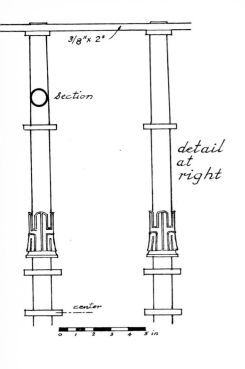

3/8" x 2"

section

detail
at
right

center

0 1 2 3 4 5 in

Wrought-iron balustrades in the *Seminario del Obispado de Guadalajara*, a men's seminary built in the seventeenth century, and now the Museo Regional de Guadalajara. That on the top guards the balcony of the chapel, while that below, on a low masonry wall, protects the open side of the main stairwell.

The balusters are similar in design. The latter contrasts a conventionalized leaflike motif above and below the three center discs with the several beehivelike turnings of the former.

A narrow second-floor balcony diagonally across from the impressive old Cathedral in downtown Oaxaca. The design of this balustrate is delicately formed with split bars, forged cone-shaped sections and discs, and further ornamented with bound groupings of "C" scrolls. The handsome, free-flowing curve of the corner brace is similarly decorated.

143

Three protective wrought-iron grilles have a common characteristic so frequently seen throughout the early city of Oaxaca, the split-bar, heart-shaped motif as their principal feature of design. The variations employed, either in the shape of the heart, sometimes elongated and sometimes compressed, or in the added minor motifs such as lozenges and "C" scrolls, gives each, when closely examined, a distinct individuality.

That on the left is exceptional. Here the craftsman used the familiar motifs with variations as where, instead of ending in scrolls, the bars terminate in small fleur-de-lis. Above, the scrolls are bound and forged to flat, delicate ends, while in the central hearts two leaves are inserted. Right, a simple *reja* is enlivened by the wavelike motion of its flat-iron cresting.

145

Home of Arturo Alonso

Above, scrolled flat-iron crestings of two *rejas* in Oaxaca. One, at a window of the Hotel Monte Alban under a valancelike carved stone, is enriched by tooled leaves. The other, on a partially demolished house, has accents of leaves and buds formed with flat iron. The intricate pattern of the pierced wood transom behind is also interesting.

A short run of iron railing has a double heart motif as its central decoration and terminates in a heavily forged newel, tulip-shaped at the midpoint, topped by an egg-shaped brass finial.

On the outskirts of Apaseo el Grande, a former *hacienda* is now a Seminary of the Order of Saint Joseph. Above, is a corner-post finial of an upper balcony. Inverted scrolls within two larger, lyrelike scrolls immediately above the rail are surmounted by four smaller scrolls to complete this unique composition.

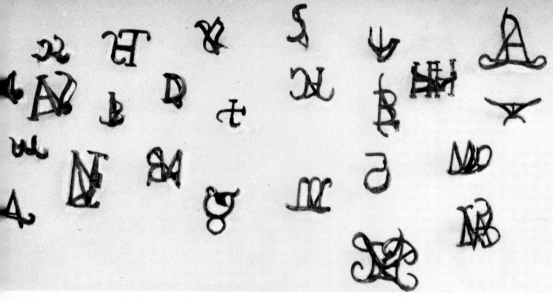

Property of Carlos & Leonardo Obregón Formoso

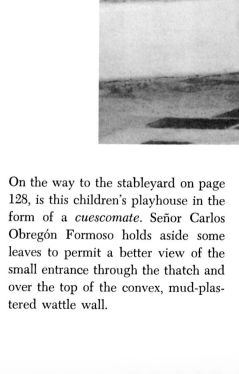

On the way to the stableyard on page 128, is this children's playhouse in the form of a *cuescomate*. Señor Carlos Obregón Formoso holds aside some leaves to permit a better view of the small entrance through the thatch and over the top of the convex, mud-plastered wattle wall.

A tempting bar retreat on the far side of the stableyard. Branding irons are embedded in the wall above a curved masonry bench on which skins of antelopes and unborn calves are thrown. Below exposed rafters ending in *pecho de paloma* outlines, a stalwart bar under a panel of bottle bottoms carries a vintage phonograph with a tulip horn. The hanging chain waits for a spigoted container of *pulque*, all ready for action.

150   A modern *Baroque* iron balcony railing, full of scrolls and elaborate designs. It is
embellished by gilded straps and richly gilded leaves whose contours are so characteristic of this curvilinear period.

Graciously curved, cantilever stones support an intricately designed wrought-iron railing in Oaxaca. Forged balusters, partially twisted between two split hearts, alternate with plain square balusters richly decorated by flat-iron bowknot designs.

Crowned by scrolls surmounted by a patriarchal cross, these simply designed wrought-iron gates stand at the inner end of the *zaguán* leading to the impressive white-walled *patio* of *Ganadería San Carlos.*

Accesorios en Decoración

Ganadería San Carlos

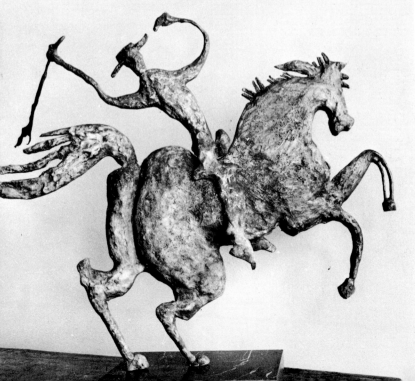

Bronzes by the young Mexican artist, Efram Vivar, are a proper introduction to a *hacienda* devoted to improving the breed of fighting bulls for the rings of Mexico. Slightly more than two-dimensional, the charging bull is about twenty-three inches overall, while the prancing horse and rider are only some eighteen inches long.

153

Two richly carved wood frames, the lower gold-leafed, whose mirrors reflect chandeliers of unusual interest. The upper is over the fireplace in the long, high-ceilinged banquet hall. Below, a frame forty-eight inches wide by sixty inches high is over the sala mantel.

Opposite, a view of the *sala* through the arch of the anteroom leading to bedrooms. At the far end, doors similar to those on page 85 give on the *comedor*, while immediately to the right are the portraits on a following page. Scale and simplicity are the commanding features.

The following legends are painted at the bottom of each matador's picture.
Upper: *Bernardo Gaviño en unison de Rodriguez "la Monja" Inauguró en Funcion Estraordinaria la Plaza "El Paseo Nuevo" el 25 de Nov de 1851.*
Lower: *Mariano Rodriguez "La Monja" Inauguró la Plaza "El Paseo Nuevo" el 25 de Nov de 1851. Resultando Herido por una res de 'El Cazadero'."*

Instead of the typical painting, here, stuffed pheasants, a hunting horn and an old gun, sportingly assembled, add color to a wall of the *comedor*.

A hand-hooked *torero*, in white and gold on a field of shocking-pink by "Mondello" has a kindred interest in the development of the fighting bull by this old *hacienda*.

The tower room, from which views of the valley, north and south, outline the ruggedness of the countryside, is reached by a circular masonry stair. Forged-iron headboards and a console are smartened by plaid blankets and the oval, tin-framed three-dimensional pictures of local wild life.

Ganadería San Carlos   *Casa Yara*

158   A soft-colored picture of the Virgin Mary, in velvet surround, framed in gilded wood, with her monogram forming the central motif of the floral topping.

It seems appropriate to find an iron bedstead of Chinese manufactory in the City of Puebla, Mexican home of the mythical Chinese princess, *la China Poblana*. The metal members, painted black for the most part, support a side rail on which charming little scenes of Oriental life are executed in gold over panels of subdued blues and greens. Empire in feeling, it is crowned with an unusual tester and curtains of rich yellow silk.

Casa del Alfeñique

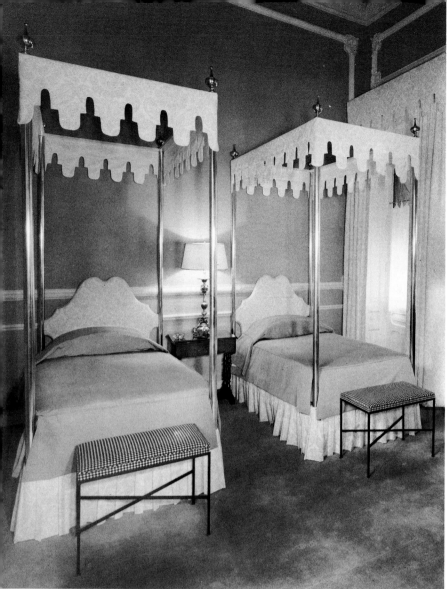

These intriguing, high-post bed-steads whose antecedents were so popular in Mediaeval times, continue to appear in modern Mexico.

A stylized conception with bright brass cylindrical posts. The pink cotton damask of the open tester is repeated on the shaped padded headboards and the pleated bed ruffles.

Home of Victor M. Villegas

Arturo Pani, Designer   *Photograph by Guillermo Zamora*

The bedsteads at the right, with their spiral turned posts and bedhead spindles, are reproductions of a seventeenth-century Spanish design of the Portuguese type. Crafted in Guanajuato, they were sent to Mexico City for the application of gold leaf, and are now returned to their city of origin. The geranium bowl of the Victorian hanging lamp adds a glow of color above the soft, fuzzy golden bedspreads and the geometric design of the white tester with its puff-ball fringe.

160

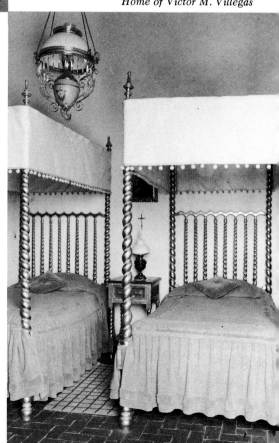

Here, a Baccarat chandelier looks down on the white flounces of a tester bed of recent design. Wood knobs, moldings and white flutes of the oyster-green posts are all accented with gold leaf. The headboards with their golden rosettes form backgrounds for the off-white bedspreads handsomely embroidered in blues.

A shaped headboard in the Spanish style of the later seventeenth century. On a field of old blue-green, the molding in dull gold leaf, forming a modified outline, surrounds a Frenchlike fantasy of blithe bouquets, garlands and scrolls around a garden fountain, painted in salmon-pinks and gold.

Home of Matilde Holbert

Another shaped headboard. The vigorous curves were inspired by the artistry of
China, brought to Europe by the early Portuguese traders. On a rich Chinese-red
background, an airy design of birds and foliage is worked in gold.   163

164   Over a bedspread of seductively soft mouton skins in light beige and two part columns for side stands, a seventeenth-century arch of gray *cantera* encloses ecclesiastical stone plaques carved in deep relief.

A former cancela of cedar with soft waxed finish, sixty-nine inches wide, is the decorative feature of the bedroom. Its regimented turned spearheads provide an austere feudal effect which is lightened by the double tier of balusters.

Villa Montaña

166   One of two headboards, fabricated in Mexico, which are reminiscent of the exquisite works of filigree found in the ancient tombs of Monte Alban. The single and double twisted brass wires form patterns which would delight any Victorian penman.

Under a concave domed light in the lobby ceiling of the Guadalajara-Hilton, a flight of twenty-five brass and copper birds move with every slight current of air. Made from light sheet material, the wings are tooled in diaper pattern while the pleated tails are similar in design to the paper tails of the bespangled white eggshell birds so popular in Mexico.

A pine buffet with curved end cupboards is decorated with lozenges formed by applied half-rounds. Of unknown origin, it was found in an old *hacienda* by its present owner, whose husband added the carved wood shell in the broken pediment.

Home of Mrs. Harry Mohlman

Two *conchas* of gracious design are separated by an acanthus-leafed corbel. The unusually fine examples of copper-luster pitchers, dating from 1830, recall the color of the broken-front drawers and the shaped panels of the doors below.

On the left, *La Virgen*, crowned by a brass nimbus, is robed in rich, Indian-red and gold *estofado*. Faintly suggested tears fall from her glass eyes.

Under a shell whose flutes are dark gray with convex surfaces in orange-yellow and against a background of soft-lemon-yellow, a sorrowing figure.

Above a dado, this floral design in orange-reds is outlined in soft grays.

A window *concha* in the outstanding *Baroque* home of the Chavolla family in Apaseo el Grande, completed in 1789 by a group of imported European artisans. Here, a face molded in bold relief with hair upswept, peers down from this crisp and dramatic conceit in marbleized plaster.

Home of Mrs. Harry Mohlman

In a kitchen niche, the shell-like motif in pink with pineapple in light green were hand-molded. Extravagant paper flowers, illuminated by an electric bulb concealed in the pineapple, are in white, yellows, pinks and turquoise. Primarily designed for carnival times, the center of each flower is an eggshell filled with confetti.

The niche below is one of a pair in the *sala*, painted white against Eden green walls. It was found on completion that the exaggerated scroll of the hinge was still not large enough to hide the light source. To do so, it was necessary to add the five leaves as a cresting.

quiet and unruffled with colors used light-heartedly

An entrance door whose chiseled surfaces give an air of antiquity has an unusual arrangement of raised panels. In over-all tones of green, it is similar to one of the doors in the Mexico City home of the noted designer, Raymond Loewe.

Home of Vernon Moore

Three views on these pages picture the same foyer. That on the right looks into the *sala* over a terrazzo floor of white onyx chips with a central Sun motif in black marble chips. Immediately below is the interesting furniture treatment of the right-hand wall. Youthful caryatids support the ends of a heavily gilded credenza-

like piece on which stand a richly ornamented, carved wood Mexican Madonna and two brass altar pieces of French lineage, partially reflected in the unique triple mirror. And left, looking backward, the mixtilinear arch of Moorish ancestry outlined by a rounded plaster nosing is shown in all its refinement.

A chair made in Mexico with its stenciled "horns of plenty" on the middle rail, closely resembles the still popular Hitchcock chairs manufactured in Connecticut starting with the second quarter of the nineteenth century. The major difference is that the base color of the original was usually black, whereas this copy is painted flamingo.

A ribbed console supports the simply molded mantel shelf below gold-leafed carved wood sconces and a mirror in an unusual frame. With light-blue walls and a white terrazzo floor, the green sofas flanking the fireplace are complemented by the sulfur, pinks and cherry-reds of the silk-covered pillows.

On another wall of the *sala*, the golden rays from a quartrefoil-shaped mirror closely resemble the familiar symbol of the Trinity. Below on a chest of antiqued green-gray with rectangular, splayed mirror panels, a charming fantasy in Portuguese porcelain of strong Oriental influence is aligned with cutglass doorknobs.

In the informal dining room, shelved cupboards are protected by doors of rare naïveté; below is a new pair inspired by the originals. One of the latter, probably from an early Zacatecas monastery, is shown opposite. On it, together with other incised motifs, the artisan shows a mitered bishop with hands clasped in prayer below a cloth bearing a man's features, possibly inspired by the Hans Memling painting of St. Veronica's attribute. The doors, first stripped, were finished in a coat of white, two coats of apricot and, lastly, a partially rubbed-off coat of green to produce a weathered olive color.

Home of Vernon Moore

A tormented clown by Jesús "Chucho" Reyes Ferreira; red hat, white face, cherry-red mouth, magenta ruche and black-streaked orange sleeves, all add to the stark drama.

A bizarre horse in shocking pink with shade lines of black. Painted in gouache on yellow china paper with a black field, by Señor Reyes.

The home of Ernesto Cervantes in Oaxaca is a privately owned and maintained museum of discrimination, housing unusual furniture and artifacts of the Colonial era. On the opposite page is a corner of the *sala*. The old, much-used table, with its shaped and carved legs, carries a collection of native ecclesiastical figures under a former wood altar-front of exceptional elegance. In it, surrounded by *Churrigueresque* conceptions, carved to a depth of about three-fourths inch, Juan Diego holds in his *tilma* the roses gathered at the bidding of the Virgin Mary. Later, when opened in the presence of his Bishop, it was found that the cloak bore the now well known picture of *"Nuestra Señora de Guadalupe,"* patroness of the Americas.

Home of Matilde Holbert

Here, identical right- and left-hand cabinets rest on a two-door cupboard which, in turn, is supported on a shaped and carved skirting with large ball feet. Curiously, the two carved designs of the upper panels are not repeated below.

184

Home of Arturo Alonso

Again the Moorish tradition is evident in the small panels of this cabinet with their carved, scroll-like designs. Saint Anthony, holding the Christ Child, stands in the niche above, a rare example of the wood-inlay work from Puebla, "*Marquetería Poblana.*"

A recently assembled *papelera* in the workshop of Giorgio Belloli. The two tiers of drawers are separated by a tabernacle, all old and all heavily gold-leafed. The painting of the Redeemer within its narrow but lavish frame is in Renaissance colors of Venetian reds and blues. The drawer fronts with their elongated motifs were originally parts of panels in an old altar.

"In the fifteenth century, it is said, the artificers of the little town of Vargas or Bargas near Toledo devised a kind of cabinet better than any of the chests or hutches previously known, and so justly famous it became that the name of the town in adjective form — *vargueño* or *bargueño* — was thereafter attached to cabinets of this type to denote their style and peculiar combination of merits."

The Practical Book of Italian, Spanish, and Portuguese Furniture, by Harold Donaldson Eberlein and Roger Wearne Ramsdall

Fitted with drop handles for easy carrying, a simply decorated exterior of incised carving, with finely fretted iron mounts, this vargueño is supported by a table of Renaissance influence instead of the more usual "H"-shaped trestle stand.

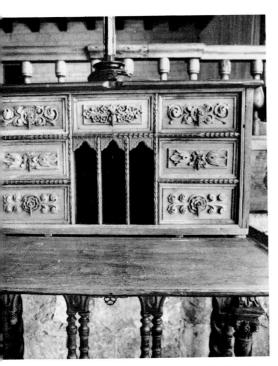

Villa Montaña

The front of a vargueño is hinged at the bottom. When swung down, it forms a writing shelf and discloses the customary tiers of three shallow drawers, which, in later examples, were combined with a pigeonhole. It was on the interior that the maker lavished his skill, either inlay or in carving, as here.

An old Mexican cupboard, seventy and one-half inches high by thirty and one-half inches wide and twenty and one-quarter inches deep. The *margaritas* of the raised panels and the running leaf design of the rails and stiles are formed with inlaid bleached bone.

Artes de Mexico Internacionales, S.A.

Villa Montaña

Above, a cabinet twenty-six and five-eighths inches wide, whose finely reeded wood panels are further decorated with roughly forged iron spike-heads, stands on a separate table.

Villa Montaña

The Madonna in unfinished wood is placed on an extravagantly carved and gold-leafed stand. On the right a turned wood candlestick in earth colors — red, green, blue and orange. Most impressive is the *Cristo* above.

The intricately pierced lock-plates on these chests are markedly fine, particularly the one at right with its interlocking vine motif.

Home of Ernesto Cervan

Chests, regarded as indispensable pieces of furniture in the earlier days, for the storage of household goods and clothing, continue to retain their popularity. These two were somewhat similar in their original decorative treatments with inlays, known as "*intarsia*" work. Above, the inlays have fallen out, leaving an interesting, recessed, geometrical pattern, while on that opposite, the differing shaded, endwood inlays are in perfect condition.

190

Embossed and incised silver, rich in Mexican symbolism, forms a bracelet from which hang masses of silver bells. The sound resulting from any motion is quite similar to that from the gravel-filled small cocoons bound above the ankles of the "deer" in the famous Yaqui Deer Dance, as he futilely tries to evade the *pascolas*.

Renaissance-type lemonwood chest with simple wrought-iron hasp and large pierced lockplate. The squares of the diaper pattern, in shallow relief, each containing an identical flower, cover front, ends and lid. Recently purchased by Robert Powers for his future Cuernavaca home.

Galería "Trini"

1.

2.

3.

4.

5.

6.

7.

DOOR STRAP DECORATIVE ENDS

1 San Miguel de Allende, Gto.
2 "Hierros Coloniales en Toluca"
   by V. M. Villegas
3 San Miguel de Allende, Gto.
4 "Hierros Coloniales en Toluca"
   by V. M. Villegas
5 Marfil, near Guanajuato, Gto.
6 Morelia, Mor.
7 Mexico, D.F. (Brass)

Amid a bewildering collection of magnificent old pieces in the storeroom of the Belloli home, a *Santo Niño* is here placed on a Tabernacle. On his head he wears a brass *potencia*, symbolic of the Trinity, while on his tunic is painted a cross and other motifs indicating that he had a premonition of his early death.

The Tabernacle from an old Indian church is abnormally large, thirty-seven inches high. Barely discernible on the blue-green door is an over-all pattern of small incised squares. The Monstrance between grapes and ears of wheat are all carved in relief and richly gilded.

Home of Giorgio Belloli

Looking through the sharply turned spindles of the organ-loft balustrade toward a golden sanctuary. This vaulted church is part of the sixteenth-century fortress-like Dominican monastery at Yanhuitlán, State of Oaxaca, now undergoing a note-worthy restoration.

Treasured is the rare twisted column of wood, the *Salomónica*, frequently enhanced with foliage. Attributed to the Baroque, when vigorously curving line and swelling form dramatized this decorative style.

In the Augustinian Convent, La Parroquía, of Yuriría are preserved these splendid seventeenth-century examples. A carved wood fragment of *Padre Eterno* and columns of the sixteenth century were rescued from the fire of 1814.

Pierced Acatlán black pottery jars make for unusual garden lighting.
Below, the white Taxco doves are carved from a balsalike wood, light enough to
be members of a small mobile.

The Guadalajara-Hilton

A rich brown door with flat, recessed panels in a convex white wall opens on the *patio* cocktail terrace. The flowers, such as the dahlia and poinsettia, pictured in many refreshing colors, are all native to this *Tierra Florida*.

The Guadalajara-Hilton

Interwoven varied widths of red-and-white striped canvas, protected by a glazed roof, add brisk gaiety to this area adjoining the pool and garden.

"... on one side ... stands the former residence of the Marquis de la Villa del Villar del Águila, the public benefactor who built the great aqueduct.... His house is an exceptionally fine example of *Baroque* seignorial mansion with great open arches on the street level and lavishly carved stonework around the windows and on the cornice above; while a frieze of glazed tiles adds an interesting band of color to the gray stone. The richly molded balconies of the second-story windows support wrought-iron railings of unusually intricate and delicate workmanship."

The Story of Architecture in Mexico, by Trent E. Sanford

A small, handsomely treed plaza in Querétaro, known as the Plaza de la Independencia, is bordered by two-story Colonial homes of elegance.

The arcade, fronting on the Plaza de la Independencia, terminates at its southwest on this narrow street with its pockmarked walls. The draped curtain effect under the small balcony ends in a carved stone pineapple, the symbol of hospitality, while through the broken light of the door above can be seen the gracefully shaped head of an old interior blind.

The street lamps of Querétaro vary in design, but all are akin because of their graceful brackets.

Here are two of the many exciting architectural features so unpretentiously displayed in the old city of San Miguel de Allende. The gadroon edging, above, frequently found on handsome English silverware, outlines the balcony floor above its elongated fluting.

Right, a scrolled pediment is broken with the familiar motif of triple pendants while plaques of geometric outlines decorate the shaped surround. The walls, now showing the many coats of previous painting, yellows, pinks and green-blues, form a pleasing background for the brown *cantera* trim of the door and of the overdoor composition.

Home of Pedro Vargas

A feature of this arcaded terrace is the ceiling. A Guanajuato family is said to have kept the secret which enables them to construct shallow, vaulted ceilings without the use of temporary forms. The salmon-colored brick arches give a wide prospect similar to that on the following page.

On *Real Salida* to Querétaro, the downhill side enjoys the advantage of a panorama of San Miguel de Allende and the country beyond from all levels.

This is the lower level of such a home. The dining terrace, with its scalloped metal canopy shielding the canvas curtains, and the flagged open terrace, with its pool on the far right, overlook still lower terraces, gardened and flowered.

Home of Eric Nören

On the upper side of a *barranca*, this two-storied bedroom wing, white trim, warm gray walls, magenta bougainvillea, looks over an *alberca* in the foreground, and, in the distance, Popocatépetl and Ixtaccíhuatl.

Home of Carl M. Stanton

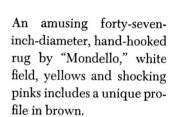

Casa Yara

An amusing forty-seven-inch-diameter, hand-hooked rug by "Mondello," white field, yellows and shocking pinks includes a unique profile in brown.

The Stanton Crest, awarded by Edward III in the early fourteenth century, is reproduced here in sheet iron, embossed by a local artisan. It forms the decorative feature of the right-hand wall.

Artesanias Regionales, S.A.

A fourteen-inch by eighteen-inch lace mat. On a natural-colored sisal field, a sisal horse, dyed black, displays its measured gait.

This lady, outlined in black iron, fifty-seven and one-half inches high, makes a most demure and accommodating bar stool with her white naugehyde-cushioned lap.

A stool supported by various sized arcs results in the form of a "Dante" chair, with a throw of black and white goatskins.

Home of Carl M. Stanton

Casa de los Tesoros

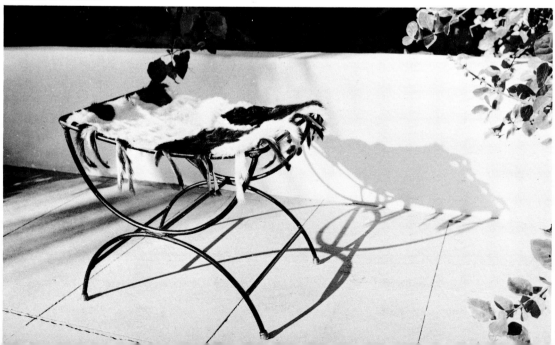

An amusing writing desk, forty-seven and one-half inches high, in structure quite similar to one of English antecedents which was on display in the Museo Nacional de Artes e Industrias Populares several years ago, particularly in its shaped apron carved to simulate a shallow valance. Made in Taxco, it was decorated by a native Guerrero artist whose abilities are usually employed in the decoration of ceramics and dinnerware. The intricate hummingbird design is done in flat black on an antique white background with gold-leafed moldings.

Two-foot adobe walls of Tubac's "Low Ruins" gallery, directed by talented Marjorie Nichols, have, at times, been part of a muleskinner's hut, the parish priest's home and a Chinese grocery. The cut-back sides of Victoria sugar distillery tins for spot lighting, an open corner fireplace with a metal hood, black pottery Oaxaca candle holders as grate sentinels, a bench by Carlos Romos below an oil, "*Sombreros*," by Marian Valentine and, to complete the Mexican atmosphere, an ubiquitous *equipal*.

Seventeenth-century Spanish tables were very like those produced in the sixteenth century. In addition to straight legs, turned or square, scrolled legs, customarily splayed, were much used.

The Mexican adaptation, in most instances, was a robust table which, because of its size and weight, required the use of two side stretchers to brace the end trestles properly. The delicately curved wrought-iron brace so often used on the Spanish originals would have been entirely inadequate. Here, patterned on the popular eighteenth-century *Baroque*, are the richly carved legs of four tables.

Casa Cervantes, S.A.

The fanciful leg above belongs to a table which was used in the home of Lic. Don Benito Juárez while he was governor of the State of Oaxaca. Again the stretchers bear carving on both sides.

A red-cedar table of about 1800 with unadorned stretchers and typical trestled legs. Their scrolled outline is heavily accented by the deep groove following each edge.

Quite different from the other three because of its size, the top only thirty-eight and one-half inches by forty-nine inches, the table above has the added feature of an apron. The raised motifs of the carving are gold leafed on a background of raspberry-pink.

The stretchers of the table on the left, with incised carving on both inner and outer surfaces, are of special interest. Again the feet are in the form of a volute, somewhat worse for wear, but recognizable.

211

Home of Jesús Reyes Ferreira

Spontaneity and joyousness are captured in a handsome old serving table. Most enchanting in color, Venetian-red boldly accented with gold, and in the rhythm of its curves. A fringed apron billows under the top with stubby tassels marking the pace. Long knee motifs from the French Baroque partially cover the modified Queen Anne legs.

El Convento, Yanhuitlán

Villa Montaña

Identical carved wood panel designs, emphasized by gold leaf on olive-green backgrounds, form the enclosing rail of the high pulpit stairs, probably dating from about 1565.

Alongside, a carved wood pilaster, sixty-four inches high, gold-leafed and very weathered, is a perfect example of the *Churrigueresque* style which inflamed the Spanish imagination during the late seventeenth century and, then, the natives of New Spain.

213

214   A portrait of Porfirio Días, after his outstanding contribution to the 1862 victory
of *Cinco de Mayo*, is hung above an unusual *caoba* stand of Empire influence.

A variant in firebox lining is this striking herringbone pattern of narrow pink brick   215
alternating with broad bands of the white mortar joints.

Below latticed doors, typically Moorish in design, large raised panels, shaped and incised to give a cushioned effect, show an eighteenth-century influence.

Santiago, with upraised sword and banner, on a prancing steed, is the focal point of this *sala* end-wall of Señor Alonso's recently completed *casita*. Below a pediment with its carved wood tympanum, this painting by a Mexican artist separates the open shelves with their upper cupboards. A simple frescoed design outlines the head and the splayed jambs of the firebox, while the fresh pattern of the back and sides is produced by slightly pillowed white cement between the exposed ends of the ordinary red roofing tile.

Without the hands, which would customarily hold certain attributes, it is difficult to identify positively this sixteenth-century carved wood figure. He was, very definitely, one of the Franciscan order, as evidenced by his robe with the short cape and standing collar and, quite possibly, the beloved Saint Francis himself. It was from friars of this order that a group of twelve, in 1524, became the first missionaries to Mexico.

The figure, twenty-nine inches high above the base, was undoubtedly carved by a Spaniard who took great care with the delineation of the head and features as well as giving great vigor to the entire composition. The costume of dark green was done in *estofado* with touches of gold.

The lampshade above is a material known as *amatl* paper. It is made by the Otomí Indians of San Pablito, State of Puebla, from the barks of various trees. Its production is limited to relatively small quantities which are in demand because of its charming, clouded café au lait color.

Home of Matilde Holbert

A provocative cupboard, whose wood is finished with a lustrous sheen blending with the willow-green walls. The play of light on the applied triangular-shaped pieces forming the design is similar to that on the facets of a diamond.

An upstairs study in the temporary home of Marcos C. de Azambuja, a high member of the Brazilian Embassy staff in Mexico. Shelves seven feet ten inches long and sixteen inches deep, are supported on cantilevered double brackets which allow for the insertion of a book. They now carry interesting articles acquired in previous tours of duty in addition to a well chosen collection of books.

Paul Barnes, a well known set designer, has used his fertile imagination in the redecoration of an old home in San Miguel de Allende. On the hood of the firebox in the *sala*, an extended platform carries a wood figure restored by Mr. Barnes: possibly Saint John the Baptist but, more likely the Good Robber who died on a cross beside that of Jesus.

A stately fireplace in an exceptionally high *sala* which is surrounded at the second-floor level by a balustraded balcony above which, against the three outside walls, bookshelves rise to the ceiling. The entablature, supported by pink clay columns with Ionic capitals and sixteenth-century-type shafts, has a broad frieze on which a Biblical excerpt is inscribed. At the left, a delicately carved Virgin with black face and vibrant nimbus.

Home of Consuelo B. de Fernandez Cueto

A flagstoned *patio* lies between an all-white entrance hall and the dining room. Bouffant curtains in white silk close the openings to each area, while potted geraniums carry their bright reds up the corners and across the low parapet to give vivid notes to the tempered emerald walls and the green mosaic lining of the pool.

Beside a recessed television cabinet and under a reproduction of an old mirror, this easel-back chair, leather-upholstered, is probably a Mexican product of the early gala *Baroque*. The wondrous carving of its front legs is excitingly unorthodox.

Home of Matilde Holbert

Home of Matilde Holbert

Between the *comedor* and the *sala*, a glass roof over the columned planting beds
and pierced center arch permits diffused illumination to highlight an otherwise
dark area.

225

Because of an ingrained preference for chests with hinged tops, chests of drawers were not widely used by Spanish peoples. Here and on the following page, however, is a masterly Mexican version in white cedar. The rippling extensions of its end panels accentuate the delicately carved floral designs of the six drawer fronts.

Home of Arturo Alonso

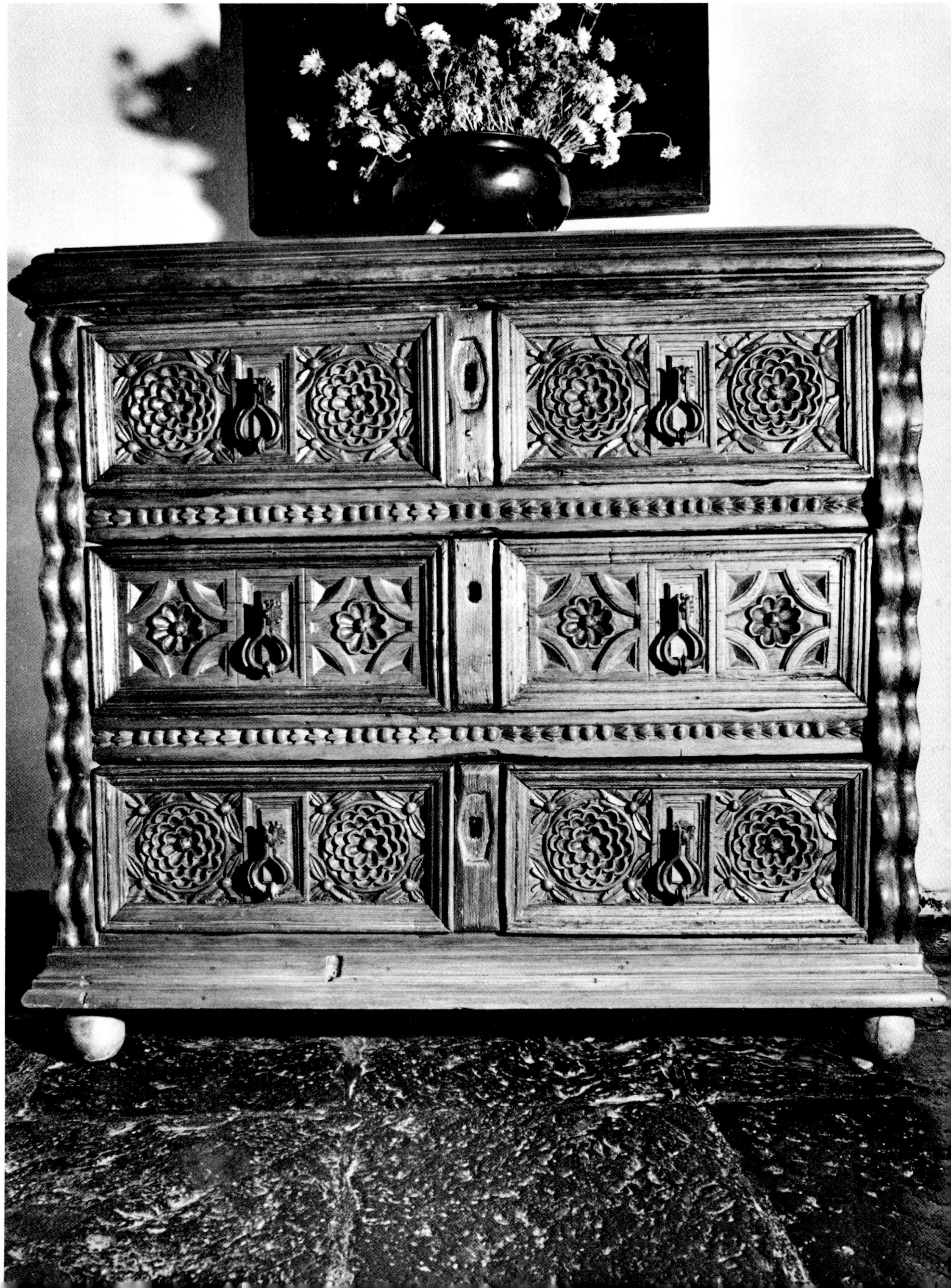

In Mexico, the lengthy regime — more than thirty years — of Porfirio Díaz, which continued into the early years of the twentieth century, is referred to as "La Época Porfiriana." During these years, the art heritage of true Mexico became hidden under an accumulation of acquired European culture, capped by the Second Empire and the Victorian, both of which matured under the Industrial Age.

Artes de Mexico Internacionales, S.A

Two proud, staunch armchairs born of this commingling of style trends, with backs only slightly canted — decorous, as befitted the times. Heavy leather-covered seats and backs, with that of the taller held by pierced *chapetones*. Arms sweep forcefully into coiled endings as they did in the Renaissance, while cabriole legs of Queen Anne lineage stand on lion's paws or claw-and-ball feet. Then, a stiffening factor is added to the normally open underseat structure — stretchers here enhance, through their pierced or scalloped outlines, this unique assortment of fashions.

The high-ceilinged executive office of an international furniture exporter. Their products, made in Mexico, are adapted from the designs of selected earlier pieces.

An *oratorio* resting on a chest, found some years ago in the small mining town of Ouro Prieto, State of Minas Gerais, Brazil. The chest evidences the influence of the French Empire but the cabinet itself is truly Brazilian. Its interior, painted blue with a scattering of golden stars, has a carved, gold-leafed *Baroque* edging immediately back of the decorated doors. The central feature, a picture of the Madonna, is exquisite.

Home of Vernon Moore

An inspiring Brazilian interpretation of the Madonna, the Nossa Senhora do
Rosario with the Christ child, each wearing a silver crown. Gay roses painted on
sky-blue fill the interior of this small, delightfully shaped *oratorio*.

231

An oil of an elegant young gentleman shows his interest in roses. Holding one in his right hand, his left wrist curves like a volute around another. The *niño*, painted by an unknown Mexican artist of the 1800s, is in subtle grays and blues against black, framed by a border of brown.

A portion of the *sala*, assured in its simplicity. The neoclassic outline of the white *cantera* mantel provides an upper shelf for the unframed painting in soft blues and Venetian red, flanked by fountainlike crystal ornaments, all above an austerely designed floor of black and white terrazzo tiles.

Home of Harry L. Stone

Home of Harry L. Stone

A massive chair, with wide flowering armrests characteristic of the late sixteenth and seventeenth centuries. Of particular note is the exaggerated headpiece, carved in the form of a shell, which crowns its back.

Brass *chapetones*, in general similar to those below, were probably used to secure the original leather covering of this chair.

A wall of *Arquitecto* Carlos Obregón Formoso's study in his Villa Obregón home. Here, the eye is attracted by many things: the heart-shaped ventilating design of the cupboard doors on the left; the use of old, carved stone fragments to form the legs and key of the firebox surround; the scale frescoed on the wall above the wood lintel for easy reference; and the various pieces of fireplace utensils. Of especial interest is Señor Obregón's collection of paintings on sheet metal in the *retablo* manner, executed by various artists but all picturing the same saint while a child, *El Santo Niño de Atocha*, whose sanctuary is in Spain.

On this and on the following page, it is easily imagined that the chairs are gossiping over their daily problems.

Above, chairs with metal tubular framing and one-piece seats and backs of white canvas, from the workshop of Giorgio Belloli in Marfil, group themselves around an old millstone table.

La Mansión

Posada de San Carlos

Around a pseudo *brasero*, these scissor-legged Mexican chairs overlook Bahía de San Carlos toward Bocochibampo Bay in the south from a gracious covered terrace. Here, their talk might well be concentrated on the too frequent repetitions of that familiar, conversational gambit, "But the one that got away must have been at least . . ."

Home of Robert Edelmann

A stone-floored dining *patio* is partially protected from the ocean breezes which flow through the rear masonry *citarilla* of the high-ceilinged, open living area to the left.

238

Home of Robert Edelmann

Winding stone stairs from the road entrance lead to the terrace level and this vast outlook over Acapulco Bay and the ocean beyond. On the left is the renowned Las Brisas area, while in the foreground a *palapa* is convenient to the *alberca* on the right but not shown.

At the left, an amusing table umbrella, scalloped and tasseled, is somewhat similar to the canvas shades of native markets. In this case, however, the wooden frame is adjustable.

239

Yalalag

The dances of Mexico are many and varied, changing between local areas and from state to state. A popular one in Oaxaca is known as the Dance of the Tigers from San Marcos. In it, boys dressed in so-called tiger costumes are roped by men as they dance about.

Actually, the painting of the costumes and masks, as that shown here, represents jaguars rather than tigers. The jaguar was used for ornamentation in the early cultures of Mexico. Priests wore cloaks of jaguar skins, and after the peoples from the higher plains of the Mexican central plateau helped capture the Mayan city of Chichén Itzá it was embellished with added constructions, one of which was the Temple of the Jaguars.

Photographs by Guillermo Zamora

Home of Jorge A. Hammeken

These conditions challenged the architect; modern design; functional planning for a family of eight — five sons and one daughter — with guest rooms and servant quarters in an older house on the property; and thirdly, the placing of a treasured reproduction of a Florentine fountain.

On land sloping up to the west, the calm façade is accented by the metal louvered railing of a cantilevered balcony. The main entrance at the rear of the carport adjoins the curtained playroom. Black, metal trim surrounds wide glass areas with lintels and bases painted gray-green between panels of smooth hard-burned brick, painted white.

Above, a part of the opposite façade; an open terrace overlooking the *alberca* and garden, with the T.V. room and fountain *patio* in the background.

surrounded by lavish
nature, a home is
interwoven by
the skill of its designers

Norman Alfe and J. B. Johnson, architectural designers

ESTANCIA – COMEDOR

GRASS ROOF

3

2

0   5   10   15   20 ft

4

5.

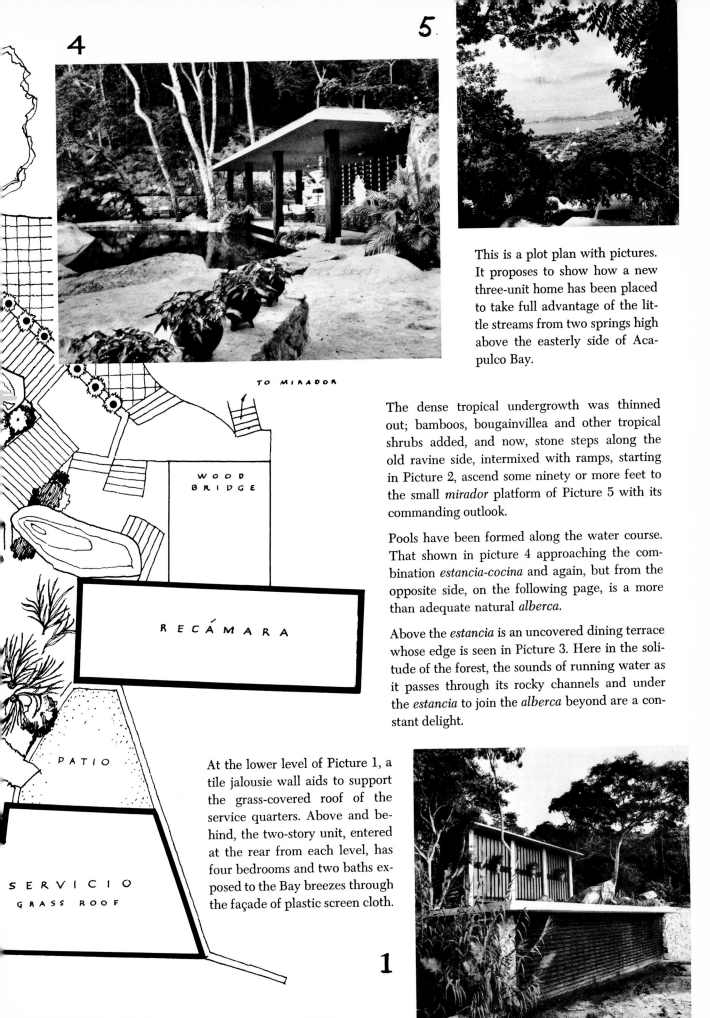

This is a plot plan with pictures. It proposes to show how a new three-unit home has been placed to take full advantage of the little streams from two springs high above the easterly side of Acapulco Bay.

TO MIRADOR

The dense tropical undergrowth was thinned out; bamboos, bougainvillea and other tropical shrubs added, and now, stone steps along the old ravine side, intermixed with ramps, starting in Picture 2, ascend some ninety or more feet to the small *mirador* platform of Picture 5 with its commanding outlook.

WOOD BRIDGE

Pools have been formed along the water course. That shown in picture 4 approaching the combination *estancia-cocina* and again, but from the opposite side, on the following page, is a more than adequate natural *alberca*.

RECÁMARA

Above the *estancia* is an uncovered dining terrace whose edge is seen in Picture 3. Here in the solitude of the forest, the sounds of running water as it passes through its rocky channels and under the *estancia* to join the *alberca* beyond are a constant delight.

PATIO

At the lower level of Picture 1, a tile jalousie wall aids to support the grass-covered roof of the service quarters. Above and behind, the two-story unit, entered at the rear from each level, has four bedrooms and two baths exposed to the Bay breezes through the façade of plastic screen cloth.

SERVICIO
GRASS ROOF

1

244

Identical black iron lanterns, ball-footed and quaintly hooded, are knowingly hung around the "Casa de Lisa," an Acapulco home.

At the far end of the relatively low loggia, four steps up, is the electric *bracero* on page 25.

The two novel ceilings of these areas are shown below. On the right, flat red tiles, painted in a white crisscross pattern, span ceiling beams laid to form a segment of an arc, while, at the left, inverted red roofing pan tile owe their effect to the alternate painting of white with the unpainted natural red.

Home of Carl Renstrom

On entering "Casa de Lisa," the stimulating view of Acapulco Bay is further enhanced by high arches of radiating, salmon-colored used brick, blending with the occasional stonework. Floors of peened Santa Tomás marble, veined with deep sage-greens, mustards, yellows and rust-pinks, add to this symphony of muted colors.

247

The Toltecs are a people of legend. Their gigantic construction works remain but their origin continues to be a matter of conjecture. Possibly descendants of the Olmecs, they left their Gulf Coast home for the southern part of the Valley of Mexico. Later they established themselves in what is now known as Teotihuacán after wandering north and east to avoid the lava flows from Ajusco. Over the years this area was built up to become the greatest of religious centers, presumably the birthplace of the Sun and the Moon.

And not far to the west is the city of Tula, probably at that time the political center of the Toltec Empire. It is thought that from Tula and present-day Cholula the Toltecs eventually returned south and east to make a major contribution to the growing culture of the Mayans. These figures found at Tula, some seventeen feet high and fully sculptured, are examples of their magnificent creative abilities.

So, before we leave this present adventure through Mexican homes, it is well to remember the many cultures on which they rest.

This latest volume in the Shipways' popular series of books on Mexican homes is a treasure trove of beauty, a book to incite the imagination. Portraying a wide variety of houses, the authors start with a unique and rarely seen *traje,* or Tarascan Indian home from the Lake Patzcuara region. Then they introduce the reader to long established haciendas, urban homes of colonial antecedents and those of ultra-modernistic design. Together, they remind one of the timelessness of cultures on which Mexican architecture rests.

DECORATIVE DESIGN IN MEXICAN HOMES is also a book of ideas for the home craftsman. It may lead him to produce a sturdy chest with old-looking straps and lockplate, or perhaps to a simpler task—gouged door panels of naive but charming effect. If paint is his medium, the addition of stylized or florid designs may be the striking result. For the home owner who wants to inject a bit of Mexican flavor there is presented a group of doors, many showing details, which may suggest a Moorish geometrical pattern, one with freer floral motifs or other possibilities.

The book's 350 photographs, drawings and plans cover a fascinating range of subjects that includes, among others, arcades and balconies, cabinets, chests and cupboards, various types of ceilings, cupolas, chairs and benches, masks and mobiles, doors, façades and entrance features, fireplaces and chimneys, frescoes and murals, ironwork, grilles and tiles, lamps and chandeliers, mirrors and paintings, rugs, wall hangings and paneling, garden walls, gates and paving, patios and fountains, kitchens and dining rooms, salas and foyers, pottery and sculptures, cristos and santos, tack rooms, bars and stairways.

This generous survey of the riches of the Mexican past and of the charm of our neighboring republic's present offers the reader a wealth of decorative meaning for his own home.